While the
BRIDEGROOM TARRIES

While the
BRIDEGROOM TARRIES

R. B. Kuiper

THE BANNER OF TRUTH TRUST

THE BANNER OF TRUTH TRUST

3 Murrayfield Road, Edinburgh EH12 6EL, UK
P.O. Box 621, Carlisle, PA 17013, USA

❧

First published 1919
This edition first published 2010

© The Banner of Truth Trust 2010

ISBN–13: 978 1 84871 067 2

❧

Typeset in 11/15 pt Adobe Caslon Pro at the
Banner of Truth Trust, Edinburgh

Printed in the USA by
Versa Press, Inc.,
East Peoria, IL

Contents

Publisher's Introduction

*T*HESE SERMONS WERE PREACHED by Rienk Bouke Kuiper in 1919, when he was the thirty-three-year-old minister of Sherman Street Christian Reformed Church, Grand Rapids. He was born in Holland in 1886 and educated at Chicago and Princeton. Sherman Street was one of the five Michigan congregations he served between 1912 and 1929. Preaching and pastoral care remained his first love, yet J. Gresham Machen drew him into the life-work of preparing others for the gospel ministry. 'R. B.', as his friends called him, was a member of the original faculty of Westminster Seminary in 1929, served as President of Calvin College, 1930 to 1933, and then returned to Westminster as Professor of Practical Theology for nearly twenty years. He preached his last sermon on May 10, 1964 and died on April 22, 1966.

For those who knew him, Kuiper was best remembered for the way he exemplified his conviction that 'a sermon is an urgent message from the living God himself'. Dr Cornelius Van Til recalled: 'When I was a student at Calvin College I was among the many students who flocked to Sherman St. Church to hear R. B. . . . He was, even in those early days, a prince among preachers.' Edmund Clowney remembered him preaching in a little house in West Philadelphia: 'Perhaps thirty people were there, counting the children, and the room was full. I can see him standing there, a little cramped for head room, preaching with dignity, power and simplicity the peace of the Lord Jesus Christ.' 'Again and again in his criticism of class sermons', Clowney commented, 'he asked, "Did this sermon preach Christ?"'

For later generations, if not known as a preacher, Kuiper has continued to be widely read. In a foreword to his last book, his friend and colleague, John Murray, wrote of 'the careful, well-balanced, informed thinking by which his preaching and writing were characterized.' And he continued: 'It is likely that *The Glorious Body of Christ* should be regarded as his masterpiece. But when the question of evangelism is so much in the forefront, it is to *God-Centred Evangelism* that the church does well to take heed.'[1]

But why reprint his earliest published sermons? And why on 'signs of the times' as he saw them nearly a century ago? One reply would be to say that what Kuiper thought of the condition of the churches in 1919 may not be irrelevant for us. The reader will find that not a few of the issues of that date are live today. 'The church wants to be big', he tells us, 'outwardly big. Big congregations, big buildings, big offerings, big statistics.' Such goals remain contemporary. He tells us that the idea of war as 'divine judgment on the human race for its sins' was 'laughed out of court' in 1919. The position has not changed.

Certainly the main subject of this book has now dropped out of public attention. If 'the signs of the times' was a popular subject in 1919, it is no longer so today. A reaction has taken place in the

---

[1] *The Bible Tells Us So* (London: Banner of Truth, 1968), p. 7, reprint pending. The other Kuiper titles mentioned here by Murray are also available from the Banner of Truth Trust: *The Glorious Body of Christ* (1966, repr. London: Banner of Truth, 1967); *God-Centred Evangelism* (1961; repr. London: Banner of Truth, 1966).

churches which was not unanticipated by Kuiper. Such is human nature that a subject which commands much attention at one time may hold little interest at another. Even among evangelicals today, while the return of Christ remains an article of faith, it can hardly be denied that interest has waned, crowded out by other subjects.

Kuiper forcefully challenges this failure in true priorities. These pages are not lectures on eschatology for the classroom but a call to awaken Christians to the meaning of the words 'the time is short'. His object is not to satisfy curiosity about the future. It is to bring the consciousness of future realities into present living — to present history as under God's control, and leading surely to a conclusion about which the world is blind.

At some points in these pages the reader may detect the dogmatism of a young man. Edward Heerema, Kuiper's son-in-law and biographer, referring to this book, says that some of the views 'held by the preacher in his early thirties underwent later revision'.[1] We may surmise what such revision might have entailed. It would have led him to drop the statement that 'the latter times', or 'the last days', refers to 'the period just before the end of time'.

It seems probable that he did not continue to regard the re-occupation of Palestine by the Jews as a fulfilment of Old Testament prophecy. In his later writings there is also a greater measure of expectation for the success of the gospel before Christ's coming, and he would criticize those who see the prospects for the cause of Christ as all dark until the Lord comes. Speaking of Romans 11:12, 15, he was to write, 'The apostle would seem to be envisaging a time when the Jewish people, who were rejected by God because they rejected his Son, will be received by God in

---

[1] *R. B.: A Prophet in the Land* (Jordan Station, Ontario: Paideia, 1986), p. 61. This is a fine biography.

mercy and will become instrumental in imparting a rich blessing to all Christendom.'[1]

If this book has weaknesses and deficiencies they remind us that caution on this subject is constantly necessary. At no point in a Christian's life does the need to 'search the Scriptures' come to an end. We remain learners, and on this subject it is love for his appearing, rather than a correct understanding, that is the mark of a Christian (*2 Tim.* 4:8). Even so, it is our conviction that the burden of the present title is greatly needed today. And that same burden remained at the heart of his thinking throughout his life.

Kuiper was too close a student of Scripture to miss the fact that living in the light of Christ's return has been the duty of believers of all centuries. As H. C. G. Moule has noted, 'All the saints of all ages are equally bidden to watch, as those who "know not what hour their Lord shall come".' So Kuiper does not write as one who believed 'the signs of the times' belonged especially to his day: 'We shall not be so foolish as to make any kind of guess at the length of time separating us from the end' (p. 53). It is not future dates we need to know to avoid being found among the 'foolish virgins' when Christ comes. But that very parable warns us, 'While the bridegroom tarried, they all slumbered and slept' (*Matt.* 25:5).

---

[1] *God-Centred Evangelism*, p. 236. The understanding expressed here is also that of John Murray, *Epistle to the Romans*, vol. 2 (Grand Rapids; Eerdmans, 1965). But Kuiper also commends the writing of Reformed authors who have a different understanding of the verses in Romans 11, e.g., William Hendriksen, *Romans: 9–11* (London: Banner of Truth, 1981), and Herman Bavinck, *Reformed Dogmatics*, vol. 4 (Grand Rapids: Baker, 2008), pp. 669–72. In addition he commends *Prophecy and the Church*, by Oswald T. Allis, who 'masterfully exposed' the errors of dispensationalism. *The Glorious Body of Christ*, p. 17.

[2] For evidence, see the concluding chapter of *God-Centred Evangelism*, 'God and the Triumph of Evangelism'.

[3] H. C. G. Moule, *Epistle to the Romans*, *Expositor's Bible* (London: Hodder and Stoughton, 1911), p. 314.

The truths needed to arouse us are all here in these pages, and no greater justification for this reprint is needed. Our age is full of inducements to spiritual slumber. The urgent response necessary to counteract that danger is the daily cry, 'Even so, come, Lord Jesus.' And until that day, the prayer must also be that Christ will continue to send preachers full of faith and of the Holy Spirit.

THE GREY HOUSE
EDINBURGH
January 2010

Preface

*T*HE FOLLOWING SERMONS were preached on Sunday evenings at the Sherman Street Christian Reformed Church, Grand Rapids, Michigan. In preparing them for the press, I did not think it worthwhile to alter them appreciably. That accounts for certain sermonic peculiarities of style and composition for which the reader desires no apology.

Though the thought of publication was not in my mind when I began to preach these sermons, no great persuasive power on the part of certain members of the congregation was required to induce me to have them published. At this particular time – the war being over[1] – a restatement of the signs of the times is necessary. Previous treatments of the subject, though not altogether out of date, are no longer up to date. Much of recent literature on related subjects is Premillenarian. We of the Reformed faith may not leave the field to the men of this school. As for the Christian Reformed people, they are Americanizing with amazing rapidity. They are no longer the isolated group they used to be. It is very necessary that they know how to take the times and the world in which they are living. In these days, when reconstruction talk fills the air, also the churches, the people of God badly need to be

[1] That is, the First World War, 1914–18.

reminded that 'the Word of God abides forever'; that 'Jesus Christ is the same yesterday and today and forever'. These are a few of the reasons why I consented to have the series printed.

The title of this volume is meant to be suggestive. Elucidation would be out of place. The phrase *after-the-war* in the subtitle requires a few words of explanation.[1] The reader will soon discover that the following pages contain much that might have been said before the war, some of it a decade or even longer ago. Yet the sub-title is appropriate. In what lies the prime significance of the war? Many answer: in the mighty changes that it has wrought. While the war did bring about great changes, yet I do not agree. *It is my conviction that the war is significant chiefly because it has given things a powerful push in the direction in which they had for some time already been tending.* So a survey of the signs of the times made in the important year of our Lord 1919, must contain much that is old.

While I beg to differ rather widely in many respects from such Premillenarian writers as Philip Mauro and Isaac M. Haldeman, yet there are many points too on which we agree most heartily. In the preparation of three or four of the following sermons I have consulted their writings, I think to advantage. Some of the quotations in 'The Consolidation of Humanity under Antichrist', for instance, are taken from Mauro's *The Number of Man*. My friend and classmate the Reverend G. Hoeksema – not a Premillenarian of course – has saved me valuable time by letting me have some up-to-date historical data which he had gathered on Zionism.

Homiletically the sermons are constructed along somewhat different lines from those to which some of those who will read them are accustomed. The nature of the subject required that much space be devoted to what may be termed 'general application'.

---

[1] The original edition had the subtitle, 'Ten After-the-War Sermons on the Signs of the Times'.

Preface

If it may please God to use this book, be it only in a small way, to lead sinners to the Cross; to help his people see some of the many pitfalls round about them, distinguish the spirit of Antichrist from the Spirit of Christ, keep active while the Bridegroom tarries, and live in readiness for his coming, I shall thank him for it.

R. B. KUIPER
1 April 1919.

I

The War

And ye shall hear of wars and rumours of wars: see that
ye be not troubled: for all these things must come
to pass, but the end is not yet.

MATTHEW 24:6

*T*HERE is a subject which is holding the attention of Christians
the world over. The world war has helped much to press it into
the foreground. It is *the Signs of the Times.* On this subject we
plan to preach a number of sermons. We consider it our duty to do
so. Did not the Saviour rebuke *his contemporaries* for not observing
the signs of *their* times, and did he not urge upon *us* the necessity of
observing the signs of *our* times?

As we commence this series of sermons, a few introductory
remarks are in order.

We shall make no attempt to exhaust our subject. If we tried it,
the year 1920 would find us still at it. In fact, it is inexhaustible.
When, on a clear night, you lift your face heavenward and attempt
to count the stars, God's diamonds, they multiply so rapidly that
you are presently bewildered. So too, if you once begin to look
around for signs of the times, they multiply so rapidly that you
soon despair of making the list complete. So we shall have to limit
ourselves. We shall consider only those signs which seem to us to
stand out most prominently today, which are written so boldly in
the sky that even he who runs can read.

Quite a number of Christian people nowadays are considerably excited about the signs of the times. Not a few show symptoms of extreme nervousness. Much literature written on the subject is largely responsible for this. But it is not right. Christians should not be excited. Christianity means peace, calmness. The purpose of these sermons will surely be to put you on the alert, but not at all to put you on the jump.[1]

It cannot be gainsaid that Christians in general are displaying a considerable interest in the signs of the times. Some leaders in the church rejoice greatly over this phenomenon. It is well. Christians today do not seem to be as blind as were the Jews of Jesus' day. That is reason for gratitude. Yet we confess that our joy is not unalloyed. It is mixed with a measure of fear. We are rather afraid that much of this so-called interest is little more than mere curiosity. Our object in preaching these sermons will not be to satisfy your curiosity. If you should be looking for that, you will be disappointed. We shall *try* to disappoint you.

Much is heard nowadays about Premillennialism. We are not going to enlarge on this subject now. In this connection we wish to say just one thing about it. If you hear Premillenarians talk, or if you read their writings, it cannot escape your notice that they like to put forth the claim of being about the only people deeply interested in Christ's return. The claim is false. You do not have to be a Premillenarian at all to take a lively interest in the Saviour's advent.

A rather serious peril besets us as we attempt to preach on the signs of the times. There is great danger that we shall try to force our personal opinions, our subjective views, upon the audience. It is almost impossible to avoid this altogether. The nature of our subject requires not merely an exegesis of portions of Scripture,

---

[1] 'Put you on the jump': that is, make you nervous, on edge, in a hurry. The phrase may have been popularized by *On the Jump*, a silent film of 1918.

but also an attempt to interpret phenomena of our day in the light of Scripture. This latter task leaves some room for subjectivism. We shall take special pains to keep sober, to stay within the bounds of unquestionable truth. We have no desire to preach anything but the Word.

Our sixth and last preliminary remark leads us directly to the subject of this sermon. *Now* is a good time to study the signs of the times. During the past five years sweeping changes have occurred on earth. The changes have been spiritual as well as material. And now that the war is over, the tumult of warfare has subsided, the smoke of battle has lifted, we ought to be able to get a fairly good perspective of present-day conditions on earth. Now, if ever, is the time to take inventory of the signs of the times.

The subject of this sermon is THE WAR. We call attention to

a.   *The war as an evident sign of the times.*
b.   *The Christian frame of mind in view of this sign.*

a. That the Saviour uttered the words of our text with a view to the impending destruction of Jerusalem cannot be questioned. The context shows it. Just as undoubted it is that he had in mind the destruction of the world, which was to be typified by that of the Holy City. For our present purpose we are concerned only with the greater of these two judgments.

In every century since Jesus uttered these words, wars were fought. Not a century has since passed the history of which does not include more wars than one. Contemporary Christians usually connected these wars with the Saviour's advent. Practically every war has been regarded by the people of God as a sign of the times. Nineteen centuries have now rolled by, and still the Lord tarries. Then were his followers always mistaken? That question forces itself upon us. If they were, then the danger is there that we may also be in error in regarding the world war just finished as a sign of the times.

The question may be answered with an emphatic *No*. The Christians of past centuries were right. For *every war is a sign of the coming of the Christ to judgment.*

Throughout the centuries, God has ever had in mind the consummation of the ages. From the creation of the world on, God has been aiming at the perfection of his Kingdom. Everything that ever occurred on earth was intended by God to hasten the return of his Son upon the clouds. Every event in the history of our race bears a direct relation to this coming event. This holds especially of whatever falls within the New Dispensation. Of earlier occurrences it can be said that they had their first end in the Lord's first advent, their last end in his second advent. Of later occurrences it must be said that they have their sole end in the final advent.

Not all events contribute in like measure to the hastening of the end. Some help more, others less. Now among those which help a great deal, probably the very first place must be assigned to wars. In war-time so very much is wont to happen. Wars create such mighty upheavals. At every war the course of events takes a big bound ahead.

And is it not true that wars must be considered judgments of God upon sinful humanity? They are always awful judgments. Surely they presage *the* judgment.

If every war is a sign of Jesus' coming, the one just ended is a very evident sign that his day is hasting apace. *This war brought it a great deal nearer.* It is that we want to dwell on in our first point.

Jesus speaks not merely of wars but also of rumours of wars. Why the twofold expression? Likely the reference of *wars* is to wars near by, while by *rumours of wars* Jesus means wars being fought at so great a distance that we hear about them only by way of rumour. It must be remembered that, when Jesus was on earth, men did not have the wonderful means of conveying news that they possess now. So the Saviour has in mind a time when there will be wars far and near, everywhere; when *the world* will be involved in war. Such a time we just passed through. The war was a world war. Never before were so many nations of earth involved in a single conflict. Involuntarily our thoughts turn to John's prophetic vision:

> And I saw three unclean spirits like frogs come out of the mouth of the dragon, and out of the mouth of the beast, and out of the mouth of the false prophet. For they are the spirits of devils, working miracles, which go forth unto the kings of the earth and of the whole world, to gather them to the battle of the great day of God Almighty . . . And he gathered them together into a place called in the Hebrew tongue Armageddon (*Rev.* 16:13–16).

And we hear Omega interrupt the vision by calling out, 'Behold, I come as a thief. Blessed is he that watcheth, and keepeth his garments, lest he walk naked, and men see his shame' (*Rev.* 16:15). While we do not assert that the battle of Armageddon has been fought, we are convinced that the world war was suggestive, even prophetic, of Armageddon.

In the context Jesus makes mention of several signs that will accompany wars. They are famines, pestilences, and earthquakes. These were striking concomitants of the past war. We all recall the mighty earthquake which, a few years ago, rocked Italy, and took thousands of lives. Two years have not yet passed since the city of Salvador in Central America was buried beneath lava and ashes, belched forth by a mighty volcano. Minor earthquakes and volcanic eruptions have become of very frequent occurrence. As regards pestilences, was not Serbia almost depopulated by the dread typhus, and has not the so-called Spanish Influenza made millions of victims in its sweep around the globe? History has again repeated itself in that disease took more fighting men than did warfare proper. And this phenomenon is all the more startling in view of the fact that the advancement of medical science and the increased murderous effect of modern weapons of warfare seemed sure to invert the ratio. How many men and women, especially how many children, died in the course of the past four years, if not directly from hunger, yet from the lack of necessary sustenance, will never be known accurately. That the actual figure would be appalling, no one doubts. Even the people of almost inexhaustibly rich America were put on rations because of scarcity of the very staff of life. Who has not thought many a time of late of the voice in the midst of the four beasts, saying, 'A measure of wheat for a penny, and three measures of barley for a penny; and see thou hurt not the oil and the wine' (*Rev.* 6:6)?

How very unexpectedly war broke out! Like a peal of thunder from an unclouded sky came the news of war in the first days of August 1914. The Universal Brotherhood of Man had become the slogan of our race. World peace was the grand end toward which statesmen the world over were striving. Governments were signing peace treaties galore. In the green meadows of quiet little Holland a splendid palace had been dedicated to peace. Naturally the number of the peaceful in Zion was being multiplied rapidly. Then, almost overnight, the sluice-gates of war were flung open, and the world was engulfed. Did you marvel? But you would not have had to marvel if only you had remembered the prediction, 'When they shall say, Peace and safety; then sudden destruction cometh upon them, as travail upon a woman with child; and they shall not escape' (*1 Thess.* 5:3). That word was partially fulfilled when war was declared; it will have its final fulfilment when the Lord comes as a thief in the night.

This know also, that in the last days perilous times shall come. For men shall be lovers of their own selves, covetous, boasters, proud, blasphemers, disobedient to parents, unthankful, unholy, without natural affection, trucebreakers, false accusers, incontinent, fierce, despisers of those that are good, traitors, heady, highminded, lovers of pleasures more than lovers of God; having a form of godliness, but denying the power thereof (*2 Tim.* 3:1–5).

How accurate a description we have here of the wickedness of men's hearts as relentlessly exposed by the war! We enlarge on but a few outstanding particulars. It cannot reasonably be questioned that one of the most potent causes of the war, at least so far as Europe is concerned, was commercial rivalry. Germany, for instance, was bending her every effort to outstrip Great Britain commercially, and the latter empire was viewing with green eyes the rapid progress of its continental competitor. Another cause was the German greed for empire, the pan-German desire to dominate the world. If we were to attempt to name the cause of the war in a single word, that word would be *selfishness*. For a long time many of us refused to believe the reports of brutish German atrocities that reached us. Though, of course, several of these stories contained exaggerations, yet many of them have been so well attested by this time as to permit of no doubt. The cruelties inflicted upon the people of Belgium and Northern France surpass description. The practices of our own American profiteers were, to say the least, scandalous. We discovered that there were surprisingly many businessmen in our land without a heart. It is safe to infer from their actions that the signing of the armistice must have grieved them unspeakably. They would have preferred to see the flow of blood-stained money into their coffers continue indefinitely. And who shall attempt to describe the triumphal parade of Venus Libentina, the goddess of sexual immorality, through Europe in the four years of war? The matter is too shameful to speak of at any length. We drop the curtain at once. Surely, the war has contributed more than a little to the filling of the cup of the world's wickedness. We marvel at the longsuffering of God. But the Judge is standing at the door. At almost any time the measure may commence to run over.

'Ye are the salt of the earth', said Jesus to his followers. He meant that Christians act as a preservative in the world, prevent its utter decay. Thus far God has spared the world for the sake of the righteous among its inhabitants. Judgment is being postponed because of the elect. But the history of the past few years indicates that this cannot continue much longer, for the simple and conclusive reason that the salt is rapidly losing its savour. The blame for the war has often been laid at the door of Christianity. Christian nations started the conflict, and to the end it remained a contest primarily of Christian peoples against Christian. It has been inferred that the Christian religion is a failure. Christianity is said to have been bankrupted. The charge is entirely false.

Yet the wording would have to be changed but very little to make it quite true. *Not Christianity was to blame for the war, but Christendom.* Because Christendom had lost its hold on the eternal principles of Christianity, the war became inevitable. If Christendom had only been more truly Christian, the war would have been impossible. And after the fight was on, the church seemed completely to lose sight of its mission. Instead of urging repentance of national sins, it stiffened the spirit of self-righteousness that had taken hold of the nations. Ministers of the gospel forgot to pray for the enemy; instead, they incited their hearers to the bitterest kind of hatred. It actually seemed that many of them, rather than have the foe see the error of his way, preferred to have him perish in his sins. Surely the earth's salt is quite unsavoury. Who knows how soon God may spew the insipid world out? To alter the figure, the corks on which the world has been floating these many centuries are crumbling. Who knows how soon it may go down?

The Word tells us plainly that the Christ will establish his perfect Kingdom when the glory of earthly kingdoms and empires shall be on the wane. That is an outstanding teaching of the book of Daniel. In the image of Nebuchadnezzar's dream the golden empire is succeeded by the silver, the silver by the brass, the brass by the iron, the iron by the divided of iron and clay. Note the descending scale! In the days of the least splendid of world empires, the stone is set a-rolling which grinds all the powers to dust, and itself keeps growing until it fills the earth. The reference is not merely to the first advent of the Son of man, but also to the second. For fully four years the glory of many world powers has been fading. While the war lasted, ministries fell weekly. Kings and emperors were deposed as if they were dummies. Erstwhile mighty empires are now hopelessly torn. And lest the rulers of the victorious nations should feel too secure, God in his providence has let loose the evil spirit of Bolshevism. The function of governments is said to be the protection of life and property. Did not the war prove this task too big for humans? It would seem to be getting time for the King of kings and Lord of lords to perfect his eternal, all-embracing government.

Zionism is in the air. By it is meant a highly organized movement planning the return of the Jewish people to Palestine. For a while it seemed that the war would prove the deathblow of Zionism. Today we can conceive of nothing that could have furthered the cause more than the war actually did. Now the Word of God tells us that at some time before the end God's ancient people will return to the land of the fathers. Many think that the fig tree in Jesus' well-known words, 'Now learn a parable of the fig tree: when his branch is yet tender, and putteth forth leaves, ye know that summer is nigh; so likewise ye, when ye shall see all these things, know that it is near, even at the doors', refers to the Jewish people. While we do not feel at all certain of that, yet we do not question that the Jewish return to Palestine will occur.

To just one more striking phenomenon we desire to call attention. According to the Scriptures, the latter days will witness consolidations on a stupendous scale. In almost every sphere of human activity, unions, organizations, cooperations, conglomerations will be effected. Has not the war led to precisely that sort of thing? The conflict began with two mighty European alliances combating each other. While one of these alliances grew but little, the other waxed until it included almost all the world.

Even America, which had always scrupulously avoided mixing in world politics, while it did not officially become one of 'the allies', yet cast its lot with the *entente* nations. Now that the war is over, a league of nations is being formed which will eventually embrace even Germany and Austria. And not only is a mighty political union being welded, but, inseparable from it, also a huge economic consolidation. With the removal of economic barriers, the world would seem destined to become unified commercially.

In an exhaustive study of the war as a sign of the times much would have to be added to what has been said. We touched upon only a few salient features. But already the consideration of these points: the magnitude of the war; the earthquakes, famines, and pestilences accompanying the war; the suddenness of the war's outbreak; the wickedness of man exposed by the war; the appalling spiritual weakness of Christendom revealed by the war; the instability of human governments brought. to light by the war; the boost which the war gave to Zionism; and the consolidation of our race resulting from the war – more than suffice to convince any Christian that the world conflict, now happily ended, has greatly hastened the coming of the day of God.

b. The practical question must next be considered, in what frame of mind we, the people of God, should be when viewing the war as a sign of the times.

Since the war is a sign of the times, it should of course cause us to look for the Saviour's advent. That is putting the matter in a general way. But in our text Jesus names several particulars.

We are told not to be troubled. Now that the war is over, it might seem needless to dwell at any length on this point. The day of trouble seems past. But is it really past? Ask those who mourn their kin consumed by Moloch! Their hearts are still bleeding; ever and anon their tears flow again. Count the widows and the orphans if you can! Follow the influenza, that deadly concomitant of war, which men find it even more difficult to banish from earth than war itself, as it continues to fell the strongest of men to the right and to the left! Visit the devastated lands of Europe! Put yourself in the place of the Russian or German or Austrian people, bleeding from a thousand wounds! Imagine what may come to pass if the contagion of Bolshevism keeps spreading! And above all, remember that, in spite of the league of nations being formed in order to render war impossible, other wars are coming. Almost every peace conference of the past has occasioned a new war. It would be a wonder if that of 1919 proved to be an exception to the rule. Did not Marshal Foch the other day predict the early outbreak of a war which, he said, would put the past conflict completely in the shadow? No, the day of trouble is not yet past. If we err not, the worst is yet to come. How necessary then that we consider the Saviour's admonition: 'See that ye be not troubled!'

We call attention to five reasons, all of them quite plainly expressed in our text, why we should not be troubled.

The wars of the latter days are predicted by the Word of God. We have that Word. We read it. Right now we are engaged in the study of one of those predictions. Therefore wars cannot overtake us unawares. We look for them. Then why should they trouble us? If disaster comes unexpectedly, men can hardly help being troubled. Then it is natural to be troubled. But if you have for some time seen tribulation approaching, when it actually comes, you are prepared for it. We Christians are prepared for the awfullest of all wars.

'These things *must* come to pass', says Jesus. He means that wars are included in God's plan of the ages. Through wars God is working out his eternal counsel. What a thought! How comforting for the child of God! God's hand directs the wars. All is well. The affairs of the universe are safe in the divine omnipotent hand. Amidst clouds and lightnings the Christian sings, 'The LORD reigneth; let the earth rejoice; let the multitude of isles be glad thereof' (*Psa.* 97:1).

As for the Christian himself, is not the God that controls the wars his Father who loves him? Does it not follow that not a hair will needlessly fall from his head, that all things shall work together for his good? In that faith his heart rests. His soul is even as a weaned child.

Wars are necessary links in the chain of events leading up to the completion of the Kingdom of God. If it were not for wars, Jesus could not come with the clouds. That too the Christian is aware of. And since he longs fervently for the King's appearance, his face beams for joy while tears of grief, occasioned by the misery of war, course down his cheeks.

'But the end is not yet.' The Saviour himself gives a commentary on these words when he adds, 'All these are the beginning of sorrows.' We thought the war was awful. So it was. But worse things are at the doors. If now already we are troubled, what are we going to do in the future? No, now is the time to keep calm. 'If thou hast run with the footmen, and they have wearied thee, then how canst thou contend with horses? and if in the land of peace, wherein thou trustedst, they wearied thee, then how wilt thou do in the swelling of Jordan?' (*Jer.* 12:5).

'But the end is not yet.' Jesus means to tell us that we should indeed be on the lookout for his appearance, but, while thus engaged, should never grow impatient. At least a few Christians did grow impatient in the course of the war. They confidently expected this to be the very last war of history. They looked for the complete ruination of the earth by it. They hesitated to pray for the cessation of hostilities. Surely, they must have been surprised by the glorious victory which the good God was pleased to give us.

Certain things must come to pass before the end will be upon us. We mention only the three referred to in the context. Jesus warns against false teachers coming in his name and calling themselves 'Christ'. This warning suggests the Antichrist. The personal Antichrist has not yet appeared. 'The man of sin' must first be revealed, 'the son of perdition, who opposeth and exalteth himself above all that is called God, or that is worshipped, so that he as God sitteth in the temple of God, showing himself that he is God' (*2 Thess.* 2:3, 4). Again, shortly before the end, the followers of the Christ will be persecuted with extreme bitterness because of the faith. Finally, the Gospel of the Kingdom must first be preached in all the world as a witness unto all nations.

With a view to these things, the Saviour desires that we exercise patience in our waiting.

Let no one suppose, however, that there is time for at least a few moments of slumber. That were a grievous error. Patiently, to be sure, but also watchfully, should we wait.

World events are moving with amazing rapidity in our age. More history is made in a decade now than has often been made in a century, possibly in ten of them. No one can say how early the three matters just spoken of as necessary precedents of the

end, may come to pass. Who can tell how soon the personal Antichrist may arise? One thing is certain: the antichristian idea of
the divinity of humanity is making startlingly rapid headway. It is
accepted quite generally by men. And might not the Antichrist, if
he should appear at an early date, expect a large following, because
of present chaotic conditions on earth? Who knows how soon the
world would lay violent hands on us if only we testified boldly
against its godlessness? That the gospel is completing its course
around the globe with almost electrical rapidity, is a matter of
common knowledge. And do not the Scriptures impress it upon
us as a matter of chief concern that we be ever ready for the day of
the Lord, because it is to come like a thief in the night, and with
the suddenness of a flash of lightning? Watch!

Finally, because these days are already so sorrowful, and because
even greater sorrows may be looked for, we should wait longingly.
The sooner Jesus comes, so much the sooner will an end be put to
the slaughter, the atrocities, the devastations of war. What Christian is not anxious for the descent of the dove of eternal peace to
flap its silvery wings over this dark earth? Who does not pray for
the early descent of the Prince of eternal peace to plant his holy
feet upon the reeking battle-field we call earth? 'Come quickly,
Lord Jesus!'

This, my fellow-Christians, should be our frame of mind: *calmly
waiting, patiently waiting, watchfully waiting, longingly waiting* for
that blessed hope and glorious appearing of our great God and
Saviour, Jesus Christ (*Titus* 2:13).

'Surely I come quickly!' Thus the Master calls out to us in his
Word, in current events, in every newspaper you pick up, in this
sermon, in the war.

Are you ready for his coming? It is the eleventh hour. Soon
the clock will strike twelve. And then will apply the most terrible
word of all Scripture: 'He that is unjust, let him be unjust still: and

he which is filthy, let him be filthy still' (*Rev.* 22:11). Before that come to pass, do give heed to another, the most .beautiful of all: 'And the Spirit and the bride say, Come! And let him that heareth say, Come! And let him that is athirst come. And whosoever will, let him take of the water of life freely' (*Rev.* 22:17).

2

The Heedless World

And as it was in the days of Noe, so shall it be in the days
of the Son of man. They did eat, they drank, they married
wives, they were given in marriage, until the day that Noe
entered into the ark, and the flood came and destroyed them all.
Likewise also as it was in the days of Lot; they did eat, they
drank, they bought, they sold, they planted, they builded; but
the same day that Lot went out of Sodom, it rained fire and
brimstone from heaven, and destroyed them all. Even thus
shall it be in the day when the Son of man is revealed.

LUKE 17:26–30

JESUS makes a comparison. He draws a parallel between the
days of Noah and those of Lot on the one hand, and the days
of the Son of man on the other.

In attempting an explanation of our text, we shall, first of all,
have to give an unmistakable answer to a very definite question.
What is the exact point of the comparison? In what particular will
the days of the Son of man resemble those of Noah and of Lot?
We might, if we chose to, draw an extended parallel and, after
considerable brain-racking, call your attention to a hundred particulars. But that would never do. We would be doing violence to
our text. The precise point of comparison must be got at.

It is quite commonly supposed that the wickedness of men is
the point; that Jesus wishes to inform us that, on his return, the
inhabitants of the earth will be as scandalously wicked as were

Noah's contemporaries and Lot's fellow-citizens. But that inter-pretation is wrong. That cannot be *the* point of resemblance. At best our text may contain a hint, a suggestion, in that direction – we believe it does – but not a single sin is mentioned by name. Eating and drinking no sane person cares to do without. Buying and selling, planting and building are irreproachable occupations. And to get married is ordinarily one of the best things a young man and a young woman can do.

The point lies in the suddenness of destruction. The inhabitants of the old world and the people of Sodom were not looking for anything of the kind. They lived in careless unconcern like that of peaceful Laish. They went about their daily occupations as if the sun would shine upon them indefinitely. Then suddenly the storm-cloud of God's annihilating wrath burst over their heads. So unexpectedly this world of ours will be destroyed. There you have the point.

But there is more to our text. We seek an explanation of this unexpectedness. Had not our antediluvian ancestors, had not the Sodomites, been forewarned of the outpouring of the divine vial? Are we not being forewarned? Pray, how then is it possible that men did not, that men do not, foresee? That question also Jesus answers. The answer is all-important for our present purpose. Let us attend to it closely. The unexpectedness of destruction of course results from the heedlessness of men. Heedlessness is the outcome, the natural outcome, of immorality and materialism. And immo-rality again is the quite natural sequence of materialism.

Materialism—Immorality—Heedlessness—Sudden Destruction; that is the logical sequence. On these four points we shall dwell successively as we compare the days of the Son of man with Noah's and Lot's.

a. That men in the days of Noah and again in those of Lot ate and drank, bought and sold, planted and builded, married and were given in marriage, was very well in itself. But the trouble was that they thought *only* of such things. These activities constituted their life, the whole of it. Their treasure was not in heaven but on earth. And of earthly things, not the higher but the lower held their interest. Spiritual things they ignored; they cared only about the material. *Materialism* was their sin.

The early chapters of Genesis tell us about the two families that peopled the earth prior to the flood: Cain's descendants, the sons of men; and Seth's descendants, the sons of God. The contrast is striking. The latter's citizenship was in heaven. Enoch, the noblest of them all, was taken up into heaven without tasting death. The former took to the earth. Cain was a tiller of the soil. He also built a city, and named it for his son Enoch. Lamech was not satisfied with one wife; he took two. Jabal became the first tentmaker. Jubal invented the harp and the organ. Tubal-cain was a metalworker. Sad to say, the two families intermarried. The contrast disappeared. The sons of God became as materialistic as their cousins.

That materialism held sway in the cities dotting the lower Jordan valley cannot be doubted. What was it that caused even righteous Lot to settle in godless Sodom? Was it not the alluring view of that luxuriant growth of waving pasture? Was it not the desire to get rich quickly? What made it impossible for him to make up his mind to flee the doomed city, so that the angels had to drag him out? What made Lot's wife turn about in her flight? Love for the things of the world. Now if even Lot fell prey, in a measure at least, to materialism, what must we think of his pagan fellows? Surely, Mammon must have been their God.

Our age is extremely materialistic. That proposition is easily proved.

Men boast of the last hundred years as a period of unprecedented progress. The world *has* progressed apace. But, mark you, not in every line, just in certain lines, especially along one line. And that line is precisely the one in which Cain's descendants excelled: *inventions.* Tents, harps, organs, metalwork, remind you of the age before the flood. The steam-engine, the steamboat, the telegraph, the telephone, the airship, the submarine, the automobile, and a million other startling inventions are descriptive of our age. Along the line of material inventions the world has made its greatest progress during the past one hundred years. That is true in a double sense. In point of inventions the last century has easily outstripped every foregoing. And the last century has witnessed more progress in this than in any other field.

We call attention to something even more phenomenal than this remarkable progress. If our fathers, a hundred years ago, had foreseen that today we could converse with one another at a distance of a thousand miles, as though we were in the same room; that one boarding the train in Chicago at 6 pm could reach New York City by noon the next day; that automobiles would race along the country-side at a speed of easily forty miles an hour; that mail would be carried by airships, outdistancing the very birds of heaven; they would have wondered how we would manage to dispose of our time. It would have seemed to them that men today would have so great an abundance of leisure hours, that they would be at a loss as to how to spend them. They would have feared that time would drag awfully in their children's days.

Well do many of us remember that, about twenty years ago, it was a standing question for debate whether the invention of all kinds of time- and labour-saving devices had to be considered a blessing or a curse; and you will recall that one of the strong arguments for the latter view was that an oversupply of labourers would be inevitable. It was feared that labouring men by the thousands would idly walk the city streets. And what is the actual state of affairs today? To be sure, the sudden ending of the war has created some temporary idleness. But in general it must be said that man never was half as busy as he is today. The rush and bustle of modern life is such that it takes a person with nerves of steel to endure it. Our age is a nervous one. Nervous wrecks abound. How can this be explained but by the mad rush of men after the material things of this transient world?

Our age may very well be characterized by the single word *commercial*. The world's commerce has assumed tremendous proportions. Commerce might fitly be called queen of the modern world. Nay, she is its goddess. And all nations pay homage unto her. For many years the world powers have been engaged in a titanic struggle for commercial supremacy. The white race exploited the other races. And it cannot be denied that one of the chief underlying causes of the great war was commercial rivalry. Commerce is the hub of the wheel of modern history, particularly of current events.

In most European countries wealth has, already for a long time, been distributed very unequally. Besides the so-called middle-class there is that of the exceedingly rich and that of the desperately poor. And the middle-class, we are told, is rapidly dwindling. In America things are tending in the same direction; since the outbreak of the war with alarming rapidity. The number of millionaires has been greatly multiplied, while the struggle for existence is daily becoming harder for the common folk. Observe how this state of affairs is bound to further materialism. On the one hand, it is true that the richer man becomes, the more insatiable is his desire for wealth. The more he has, the more he wants. And on the other hand, practically all the time and energy of the poor are needed for them to eke out a meagre existence, to keep body and soul together decently. Now, is not that a sign of the times? Precisely to this condition James refers when he warns the rich that they have heaped treasure together for the last days, and advises the poor to be patient unto the coming of the Lord (*James* 5:3,7).

b. Almost all commentators on our text find a reference in it to the *immorality* prevailing in Noah's and again in Lot's day. That may seem somewhat remarkable since, as was already pointed out, not a sin is named. Are all these expositors wrong? We take it that they are surely right.

Jesus speaks of materialism. Now he knew – and everybody who is at all versed in history is acquainted with the fact – it is a generally recognized truth, that the natural sequence of materialism is immorality. It has ever been so. Besides, the very mention of Noah's and Lot's days suggests the thought of immorality. So deeply were the contemporaries of these two men steeped in the grossest forms of wickedness, that their days have become almost synonymous with immorality. You just cannot help thinking of immorality when you hear those times spoken of.

The marriage relation was scandalously desecrated before the flood. The lust of the flesh ran wild. To such an extent was the earth polluted that it required all the waters of the flood, covering even the highest mountain peak, to wash it clean.

A like form of immorality, even a worse, prevailed in Sodom. Of the particular sin of the Sodomites, which called down upon them fire and brimstone, we catch a glimpse in the story of the angels' visit to Lot's home. Said the Sodomites surrounding the house, 'Bring out these men that we may know them.' And the unspeakable sin which Lot's two daughters committed with their father can be explained only if it be remembered that they had long breathed the stench-laden air of wicked Sodom.

Is our age immoral? That is an interesting question of great importance: a question seemingly difficult to answer, and yet quite simple. On the one hand, it would seem that the world is rapidly improving. In another sermon we hope to dwell on the present-day demand for and insistence upon righteousness in the various spheres of life. The public schools try hard to instil into their

WHILE THE BRIDEGROOM TARRIES

pupils a high type of morality. It is sometimes said – we are sure, falsely – that the morals of the public school children surpass those of the boys and girls attending our Christian institutions. The saloon is doomed. Liquor is going to be banished from modern society. Only a few years ago almost every city of any size had its segregated or red-light district, where vice flourished under police protection. Now these holes are being cleaned out. And is it not cause for great joy that our government tried so very hard, and, if we are correctly informed, succeeded so admirably, in. keeping our army and navy clean? Even now the government is carrying on an organized. campaign against venereal diseases. Surely, it would seem that the world is becoming better.

Don't let the devil fool you! He has not changed, and he still is the prince of the world. He has merely shed his coat of lion skin and assumed instead the white flowing garment of an angel of light. For the grosser forms of immorality he has substituted more refined. Just because they are more refined, they are more seductive. And so it has come about that immorality, instead of being confined to a limited number, to the roughs and toughs, has by this time pervaded almost all society.

'Satan has given up the flaring red-light streets. It does not look nearly as bad to have the red lights scattered throughout the city, big distances apart. They are attracting men of whom you would not think it. Theatres have always been looked at askance by the best Christians. Satan has decided to meet them half way by establishing a *vaudette* – just an innocent moving-picture show, you know – around the corner. Lots of nice church people go. Almost everybody blushes when the word *whore* is mentioned in public. But Christian women have long forgotten to blush as they and their daughters parade the streets in whorish apparel. It does not seem half as bad to get rid on the sly of offspring that you have never seen, as to kill a babe outright after it has come to huddle in your lap, to throw its pussy arms around your neck, to hold its dimpled cheek to your lips for a kiss. God alone knows how many mothers – no, not mothers: brutes, beasts – do the former. Hosts of women are working hard for the moral uplift of society, the moral betterment of their fellows, who themselves are too lazy and too immoral – we mean it: too immoral – to assume the duties of motherhood. The devil has put us wise to it that it is really immoral for a man and a woman to live together as husband and wife if they are not 'affinities'. That is one reason, and an important one, why the divorce courts are so very busy.

So immoral *we* are. Think of it: *so* immoral we are after the light of the Word of God has been shining on us for many centuries. Would you be surprised to see an antediluvian or a Sodomite rise up in the judgment against this generation?

c. You know some absent-minded man. You have wondered how he manages to cross a busy down-town street without being struck by an automobile. You have seen a drunk man crossing a bridge. You were held in suspense as you expected him at any moment to topple over the railing. The absent-minded man and the drunk man are in danger of a sudden and serious mishap, because both are *heedless*.

Noah's contemporaries and Lot's fellow-citizens were absent-minded and drunk at the same time. So are men today. Materialism causes absent-mindedness. If a man has his heart set on the material things of this world, he has neither eye nor ear for anything else. Immorality causes drunkenness. Every immoral man, no matter what form his immorality may assume, is drunk. Can you think of anything more heedless than this combination: an absent-minded man, intoxicated?

Already Enoch, who was translated some seventy years before the birth of Noah, had forewarned men of the coming judgment.

They had turned a deaf ear to him. Noah preached for years and years without making a single convert. He preached by deed as well as by word. He built the ark on the dry land, far away from the water's edge. Men laughed him to scorn. They likely doubted his sanity. God preached by a startling miracle. At the divine command animals of every kind flocked to the ark. But nobody took notice. Surely, that was the extreme of heedlessness.

The people of Sodom were heedless. A few years before God had visited them with a dire calamity because of their wickedness. Their foes had carried them off into captivity. If it had not been for Abraham, the friend of God, that would have been the end of them; their name would have been blotted out from under heaven. Should they not have turned from their evil ways? But they did not. May we not assume that Lot, since his righteous soul was wearied by the vice about him, raised his voice in warning? He could not keep his peace. And ought not the miracle performed by the angels in smiting them with blindness, as they sought entry into Lot's house, have awakened them to the realization that there is a God who executes judgment upon the earth? But they were too blind to see even that.

That men today are. heedless is altogether too evident. We call attention to it that they pay little or no heed to the warning voice of God as it comes to them in the Bible and in the signs of the times.

The Word of God no longer occupies the place of honour in the home that it used to. Thousands of families have no Bible; in thousands of others it is never read. The most orthodox churches have households enrolled which, if it were considered a crime today, as it was in Reformation times, to possess a Bible, would be found innocent. The good old custom of reading the Scriptures at meals is rapidly losing ground even among as conservative a people as we are. Lots of so-called Christians are completely ignorant of the commonest of Bible stories. The other day we met a man who was unable to locate Bethlehem; think of it: Bethlehem of Judæa, the birth-place of the Saviour of the world!

Does not the distribution of millions of copies of the Word of God among the men in military service and the eager reading of it by hundreds of thousands, indicate that the Bible is being restored to its former place of honour? That is a good question. We only wish that we could answer it with an unequivocal *Yes*. But can we? We rest assured that many of the 'boys', while in service, learned to believe in both the written and the personal Word. We rejoice more than we can say. But is it not likely that many who sought comfort in the Word while in distress and danger, will feel that they can do without it after having left service? Did we at home read the Bible as eagerly as did our soldiers and sailors? Is it not true that, while friends and churches and Bible Societies were distributing Bibles galore, many professors of theology and ministers of the gospel kept assailing the authority of the Book? And is it not significant that, of all the faults of Germany to which our attention was called the last few years, very likely least was said about that country's having been for several decades already a veritable hotbed of Higher Criticism?

Sunday, the Lord's day, is wont to be spent under the preaching of the Word by a rapidly decreasing number of men. Sleeping, visiting, joy-riding, and theatre-going are more and more taking the place of church-going. An epidemic comes and the churches are among the first public places to be closed. Public worship is not essential; so the authorities decree. Here let us add that we fear greatly that the past war will prove to have caused sad deterioration in the matter of Sabbath observance the world over. Granted that much work was essential on the Sabbath while the war lasted, we are afraid that, now that peace has returned, many will continue the habits which they formed in war-time.

The war is a striking sign of the times. Comparatively few think of it in that light. The great majority of men regard it from a purely human viewpoint. 'Man brought on the conflict; man ended it. That is all there is to it.' That the war was a divine judgment upon the human race for its sins – the very idea is laughed out of court. Just consider: not to see the hand of God, not to hear the voice of God, in the greatest war of all history! Is it not surpassingly awful? And if you tell men that the pestilence which has been raging on earth the past months was a sign of the times, a warning of the judgment to come, they just smile. 'You are an old fogey. God did not send the influenza; germs caused it.'

Men are worse than heedless. They are hardening their hearts. Now is a good time to preach on the mournful words of Jeremiah: 'O Lord, are not thine eyes upon the truth? thou hast stricken them, but they have not grieved; thou hast consumed them, but they have refused to receive correction; they have made their faces harder than a rock; they have refused to return' (*Jer.* 5:3).

d. History repeats itself.

Not one of Noah's contemporaries, outside the members of his family, had the slightest presentiment of the impending catastrophe. Everybody was busy about his daily work. The peasant was ploughing. The carpenter was building. In yonder house there was music and dancing. Suddenly the rain-clouds burst and the sluice-gates of the underworld were flung wide open. All perished in the waters.

The Sodomites were fast asleep. The cock had not yet sounded his morning call. Suddenly the heavens opened. Fire and brimstone consumed them all.

Belshazzar was drinking wine together with his princes and wives and concubines out of the golden vessels taken from the house of Jehovah at Jerusalem. Yes, the city was besieged by Cyrus the Persian; but that did not trouble Babylon and its king. The drunken banqueters sang: 'I sit a queen, and am no widow, and shall see no sorrow' (*Rev.* 18:7). All of a sudden a hand wrote on the wall: 'Mene, Mene, Tekel, Upharsin' (*Dan.* 5:25). That night the city fell, the king perished.

The Jews were celebrating the Passover at Jerusalem. No one thought of danger. From every quarter the people flocked to the city. The normal population of 250,000 was increased to 2,700,000. Then it was that Titus Vespasian, the Roman, laid siege to the city.

Rome was bathing in luxury,. revelling in riches, sweltering in vice, trusting in power, boasting of empire. Presently the barbarian hordes from the North swooped down upon it.

Today men are chasing madly after the material things of earth. With feverish devotion they are serving the lust of the flesh, the lust of the eyes, and the pride of life. They have neither time nor desire to think of aught else. To the voice of warning they reply: 'Where is the promise of his coming? for since the fathers fell asleep all things continue as they were from the beginning of the creation' (*2 Pet.* 3:4). They sing of 'peace and safety'. If the great world fire should *now* be kindled, would not the prophecy be fulfilled: 'Then sudden destruction cometh upon them, as travail upon a woman with child; and they shall not escape' (*1 Thess.* 5:3)?

What are we going to do to escape this sudden destruction?

First of all, get at the root of the matter! Let us take heed lest we get under the spell of *materialism*. For *materialism* leads to *immorality; materialism* and *immorality* cause *heedlessness;* and *heedlessness* is sure to be followed up by *sudden destruction*. Shall we then stop planting and sowing, buying and selling, eating and drinking, marrying and being given in marriage? God forbid! That the Christians at Thessalonica did, but Paul rebuked them for it.

But never shall we permit such activities, no matter how legitimate and even necessary, to crowd out devotional religion. Let us take time, if need be *make* time, for Bible-reading, prayer, church-going, and the like. If you neglect these duties, the goblin of materialism is going to get you.

It is just as important that we learn to serve God in our daily activities: that we learn to eat and to drink, to buy and to sell, to build and to plant, to marry and to be given in marriage, unto the honour of God; that we learn to be religious *always*. Then it will not matter, when Jesus comes, whether we are in church, or in the office, or behind the counter, or in the factory, or at the dinner-table, or in bed.

Above all, get into the ark while God's warning voice resounds and the light of the gospel shines, before black storm clouds gather and the voice of God rolls in awful judgment! Do you ask, what ark? The Ark of salvation, *Jesus Christ*. Oh, give your hand to the Angel of the Lord, the Son of God, who would lead you out of. Sodom, lest you spend eternity in the place of fire and brimstone! If you do, the Ark will bear you up to a mountain higher than Ararat; the Son of God will lead you out to a city better than Zoar: the mount and the city of God.

'And destroyed them all'; so we read twice in our text. How very few were saved! Just eight out of the flood; just four, no three, out of Sodom. Few of those living will be saved when the Son of man comes. But do not therefore despair! Rather do you strive all the harder that *you* may enter in by the narrow gate!

And if you have given your hand to the Saviour, beware of looking back at the things you left behind! Never once permit the love of the world to turn your eyes Sodom-ward! 'Remember Lot's wife' (*Luke* 17:32)!

3

The Church's Departure from the Faith

Nevertheless when the Son of man cometh,
shall he find faith on the earth?

LUKE 18:8

WE WISH TO SPEAK on *the church's departure from the faith*.
Maybe you do not see at once how our text fits our subject;
or rather, how we can derive our subject from our text. You
say: Jesus makes no mention here of the church, yet on the church's
decadence you are going to preach. Let us spend a few moments
studying the context.

Our text is found at the very end of the well-known parable of
the· poor widow and the unrighteous judge. The lesson of the parable of course is that we should be persistent in prayer. Everybody
knows that. But the parable has a deeper meaning of which not
everybody seems to be aware. The widow represents the church of
the latter day. She is being ill-treated by the world. Almost is she
being crowded out of the world. And now she lifts her head upward, longingly looking for the coming of the Lord, her Deliverer.
What Jesus desires to tell the church of the latter day is this: that
she should keep praying fervently, persistently, for his return and
her own deliverance. And he assures her that this prayer will be
granted speedily. But then all of a sudden the sad thought comes to

29

Jesus that at the end of time but very few will care to pray thus, for faith will well-nigh be banished from the earth; the number of the faithful in the church will seem negligible. And therefore he sighs: 'Nevertheless, when the Son of man cometh, shall he find faith on the earth?' Do you not see then that our text really refers to the deplorable condition of the *church* at Christ's coming?

We repeat our subject: THE CHURCH'S DEPARTURE FROM THE FAITH.

We shall mention no points, no divisions. Instead, in order to render easy the following of our discourse, we ask you to bear in mind throughout the sermon a very simple definition of *faith*. It is not that of the *Heidelberg Catechism* or of the *Compendium*. It is much shorter and simpler than either of these; necessarily it is not as full; yet it fills the bill. *Faith is belief in the supernatural.* There you have it. It follows at once that *departure from the faith means denial of the supernatural.* And exactly that is taking place in the church today on an unprecedented scale. The church is flouting the supernatural. That is going to be the one point of this sermon.

We sometimes say that we have a natural revelation of God in nature round about us, and a supernatural revelation of God in the book we call Bible. Not so very long ago, only a good century, the whole Christian church subscribed to the latter truth as well as to the former. Practically everybody was as sure of the Bible's being the infallible Word of God as are our little children in the Borstius[1] class in catechism today. What a change a single century has wrought! University professors made the discovery that there is nothing supernatural about the Bible after all. It is a book in a class with books of purely human authorship. That it is the inspired Word of God, that its authors were controlled by the Spirit of God

---

[1] Jacobus Borstius (1612–80) was the author of a catechism for the very youngest children.

so as to write infallibly, is a dogma good enough for our ancestors of the sixteenth century; but we of the undogmatic twentieth have cast it on the rubbish heap of antiquated, old-fogey ideas. If you want to, call Isaiah, John, Paul, and others inspired – it sounds good – but remember that they were inspired in no other way than Dante, Shakespeare, and Longfellow. Of course there are mistakes in the Bible, lots of them. Some of these learned men have undertaken to point them out, and the result has been that, by the knife of the so-called Higher Criticism, the whole book has been ripped to shreds worse than baby's ABC book after it gets through with it. There you have the modern view of the Bible, first propounded by university professors who thought they were wise but in the eyes of God were blatant fools; since transmitted by thousands of so-called ministers of the gospel of truth, in reality servants of the liar from the beginning; and by this time accepted by millions of church-goers, about half of which are church-goers no more.

What is the outcome? What does the rejection of the Bible as God's supernatural revelation lead to? But one answer is possible. It leads inevitably to religion without authority. And religion without authority is as gross a monster as government without authority. It is anarchy. Religion without authority is as little religion as a man without a backbone is a man. To talk about religion without authority is as foolish as to talk of building a house without a foundation. To maintain religion without authority is as impossible as to boil water in a bottomless vessel.

What influence, if any, may the war be expected to exert upon belief in the Bible as the Word of God? Since Higher Criticism has flourished especially in Germany, and German is almost synonymous now with taboo, it might be expected that men would show at least an inclination to return to the ancient faith in the infallible Bible. But the evidence does not point in that direction. You have observed – everybody has – the general restlessness that today pervades the human race. It is hard to describe. Some call it the spirit of Bolshevism, but that description is not accurate. So much can be said for sure: men are discarding the old and demanding things new. Reconstruction is the talk of the day. In so far as this includes a break with traditionalism, we rejoice. But we are very much afraid that it also means a break with well-constituted authority. The authority of the Bible too is at stake. We *know* it is. Why, even in the most conservative churches there is needed a perfectly sound reassertion of the doctrine of inspiration. The need is growing.

In the days of the Protestant Reformation, what did the fundamental difference between the Roman Catholics and the Protestants consist of? Simply of this: while the former recognized, besides the authority of the Bible, also that of tradition, of the church councils, and of the pope, the latter flatly rejected all authority except just that of the Bible. The sole and therefore the absolute authority of the Bible, that is the foundation of Protestantism. But now behold that foundation crumbling! It is crumbling rapidly. If it keeps crumbling much longer, it will be gone; and great will be the fall of Protestantism.

In some parts of the Bible the supernatural seems to play a greater role than in others. Most boldly does it stare the reader in the face in the narration of the miracles. The miracles strike us as being the height of supernaturalness. Small wonder that the unbelievers in the church and without direct their first and most forceful attacks on the miracles.

Just let us illustrate how they try to go over the top.

The Word of God tells us that the prophet Elijah was taken up to heaven bodily in a fiery chariot drawn by fiery horses. Of course it cannot be true. Nature knows of no law that would permit of such an event. The law of gravity rules it out absolutely. But then what did happen? Very likely something like this. One day, while out for a walk, the prophet was overtaken by a thunderstorm. It was a severe storm. Elijah was struck by lightning. He never got over it altogether. He recovered only in part. He remained a life-long lunatic. That accounts for his wearing such strange clothes. That is also why you read so many weird stories about him.

The Reverend Isaac Haldeman is authority for the following illustration. A seminary professor and his class had come to the story of Jesus' walking on the waters of the Galilean sea and Peter's attempt to do the same. 'It goes without saying', said the professor, 'that Jesus did not actually walk on the water. The laws of nature would not have permitted it. In reality Jesus walked on the shore. A mist had risen to about the height of the knees, and so it looked to the disciples in the boat as if he were walking on the water.' A bright member of the class interrupted: 'But Professor, how do you explain that Peter sank when he tried to walk up to Jesus?' With a condescending smile the teacher replied: 'They were near the shore. The water was not very deep. It was filled with long sedgy grass. As Peter stepped out, this grass held him up. He thought he was walking on the water. Then he suddenly lost his nerve and imagined that he was sinking.'

We come to more important matters. And now the thing becomes extremely serious. Stop smiling! You have more reason to weep.

The creation of heaven and earth was a miracle. It is flatly denied. The theory of evolution is substituted for it not only in the schools, but in many churches as well. So the Bible begins with a lie. But that is a bad beginning. A book that *starts* with a lie is quite sure to contain lots of them. And so we would advise you to throw your Bible into the wastepaper-basket for future use in starting a fire rather than to turn over a single leaf.

The Saviour's virgin-birth was a miracle. For that very reason it is said to be false. No, Mary was not a virgin when she gave birth to her first child; she was a fallen woman of the kind they receive at the Evangeline Home on East Fulton Street in our city. And Jesus, far from being the natural Son of God, was the illegitimate son of nobody-knows-whom. Tell us, if your preacher had the boldness to proclaim such things, would you not drive him off the pulpit and out of the church? But be assured that even in as good a church as the Presbyterian there are several ministers who preach precisely this doctrine, though perhaps not as bluntly as we put it. And the wonderful thing is that the church just named has confessions every bit as sound as those of our Reformed churches. The Westminster Confession is a masterpiece of orthodoxy.

The incarnation was a miracle. That the eternal Son of God assumed human nature is the miracle of the ages, the miracle of all miracles. For that very reason it is violently assailed. 'Surely,' says the modern minister, 'Jesus of Nazareth was the Son of God. But so are you God's son and so am I. All men are God's children. The remarkable thing about Jesus was not that he was God's Son, but that he discovered the great truth of the Universal Fatherhood of God. But that he had existed from eternity as the second person of the Trinity is theological junk.' Now let us assure you: either Jesus was the eternal Son of God, or he was the biggest impostor, the grossest deceiver, that ever trod upon the earth; for he said: 'I and the Father are one'; and again, 'Before Abraham was, I am.' If the modern preacher is right, then the Jews were right in demanding for Jesus crucifixion; if I had been present on Gabbatha that memorable Friday morning when the Nazarene was tried by Pontius Pilate, I too would have yelled at the top of my voice: 'Crucify him! Crucify him!'

The resurrection of Jesus Christ from the dead was a miracle. It is denied. Or rather, it is interpreted in such a way as to get around the miracle. Jesus' body of course remained dead. What is dead cannot come back to life. But in a spiritual sense the Master was resurrected in the hearts of his followers. When Jesus died, they were downcast. They were on the very verge of despair. But on Sunday morning, following the crucifixion, the spirit of Christ – whatever that may mean – revived them. They took courage. They got a new lease on life. For they knew that, though the Master's body was gone, his soul was marching on, just as in the old song the soul of John Brown is said to be marching on. Now listen! If Jesus is still dead, then he is not in heaven today, and then he will not appear upon the clouds tomorrow. In tears I complain with Mary Magdalene: 'They have taken my Lord.' He is gone. And if he is gone, my present is ruined, and my future, which I thought was as bright as the city without night, becomes dark as hell.

We speak of no more miracles. Enough has been said to make it plain that to deny the miracles of Scripture amounts to blowing the very bottom out of Christianity. Get rid of the miracles, and Christianity has vanished like a mirage in the desert. And in a desert you are. Yet comparatively few teachers at theological seminaries and ministers in Christian pulpits take the miracles seriously.

The devil is a superhuman person. Large numbers of Christians so-called deny that he is a person at all. Only the extremely conservative still believe the existence of a personal devil. The modern minister of the gospel laughs him out of court with laughter so violent that he almost rolls over. It might be supposed that Satan would feel hurt about it that men refuse to recognize even his existence. *We* do not like to be ignored. But not so the devil. Nothing pleases him more than to be ignored. For now he can do to men almost what he pleases. He can play rings around them. An enemy to whom you close your eyes is sure to overwhelm you. There then we have one of the chief reasons why the father of lies is so rapidly gaining control over the church. It is simply because an ever growing number in the church ignore him. And when the minister laughs about the devil so that he nearly rolls over, the devil laughs ten times louder so that the very walls of hell reverberate.

The sinner's salvation from beginning to end is a supernatural process. More plainly put, the salvation of a sinner is the work not of man but of God omnipotent. That is a fundamental of Christian doctrine. By nature man is spiritually dead; not merely ill, not merely very sick, not merely dying, but actually dead. Who ever heard of a dead man's coming to life by his own power? That is an utter impossibility. That were a contradiction in terms. No, God alone can bring the dead to life. He does so in regeneration, the birth from above, the supernatural birth. Now the sinner stands on the way of life. And for each succeeding step that he takes, he is as deeply dependent on God as the branch is dependent on the vine for life. Faith, conversion, sanctification, are all of them supernaturally wrought. And then, how strikingly the supernaturalness of salvation appears in the very last step, glorification at the resurrection of the body! Surely, it requires the voice of God to call forth the buried from their graves, the drowned from the depths of the ocean, the cremated from the four winds.

The modern preacher denies the supernaturalness of man's salvation. Wisely he begins by rejecting the doctrine of total depravity. Full well does he realize that this stumblingblock must be removed first of all. If it remains on the road, no progress can be made at all. If only it is cleared away, ,he will henceforth have easy travelling. So he says that man is not by any means spiritually dead. There is something good in every man, a spark of divinity, if you please. It is for man to fan that spark into flame. It is man's task to develop the good that dwells within him. To use a modern phrase, man must come to *self-realization*. And if only he attempt that with a will, then, without a particle of aid from the God of our ancestors, he will advance from strength to strength until he arrives in Zion.

'Ah,' you say, 'but how about the resurrection of the body? Does the modern preacher put forth the claim that man can raise his own body from the grave?' That question angers your up-to-date minister. Knowing that he cannot give a satisfactory answer, he knits his brow. He is cornered. But he is far too proud to admit it. Now he has regained his composure. With a condescending smile he, the man of scholarship, informs you, child that you are in knowledge, that there never will be such a thing as a resurrection of the body. With a single breath of his lips he blows the problem away. Unable to solve it, he destroys it.

And now we ask: what is left of Christianity if the modern preacher is right? We answer: precisely nothing. He casts all of real Christianity before the moles and the bats. Again we ask: what comfort can be gleaned from such a gospel; what satisfaction can it give? Once more we answer: none at all. As our eyes grow dim with age, as the night of death approaches, it gives no vision of a city the gates of which are not closed by day because there is no night there. When we stand at the entrance of the valley of the dark shadows of death, peering after a dear one who has just entered, it can do no better than ruthlessly rob us of all the sweet stories of heaven we learned at mother's knee. As we entrust a beloved body to the grave, where presently perfect darkness will reign, it offers us not the faintest ray of light. The new religion gives us for bread a stone, for a fish a serpent, for an egg a scorpion. Its outcome is black despair.

We come to an important matter. That the new-fangled preacher takes from us the supernatural religion of the Bible has become sufficiently plain. Now the question arises, what he gives instead, what he has to offer in the way of a substitute. The answer must be: but little, but very little. Much of his time he wastes in attempting to make the supernatural religion ridiculous. He has little time left for anything else.

But that little, what is it? We call it the *gospel of human righteousness.* Let us explain.

It cannot be denied that there is among the Christian peoples today a general and insistent demand for righteousness. The air is filled with cries for international righteousness. We have just finished fighting for this noble cause against a government which seemed to lack all regard for righteousness. In the decade preceding the war volumes were written on the subject of civic righteousness. Everywhere we meet an insistence on righteousness in personal life. Business is no longer humbug; the business man who would succeed must be honest in his dealings. In a word, all the powers of Christendom are banded together 'to make the world a decent place to live in'. Who does not rejoice?

But now observe! The modern minister has made this righteousness his subject for the pulpit. It is his hobby. Briefly put, he preaches only morality sermons. Very plainly put, his one theme is: 'Be good and do good.' Now listen! That is radically wrong. His one theme should be quite another. It should be that of the greatest of the apostles. Said he: 'For I determined not to know anything among you, save Jesus Christ, and him crucified' (*1 Cor.* 2:2).

Mark the contrast! The modern gospel is that of a Jesus who merely gave us an example of good living; the true gospel is that of the Christ who died on the tree in sinners' stead. The modern gospel tells us that by being good and doing good we can draw nigh to God; the true gospel tells us that the only way of approach to God leads by Calvary. The modern preacher calls the true gospel the theology of the butcher-shop; we call his gospel the theology of the Ladies' Literary Club.

We wish to make a statement here that may surprise some Christians. However, we are confident that a brief explanation will end their surprise. The devil would not mind if every saloon on earth were closed within a week; if every house of ill fame were burned to the ground together with the inmates, today; if, by the time the peace-conference, now in session, has completed its work, this world should be a far more decent place to live in than it ever has been.

Now do not misunderstand! We Christians should not favour the saloon. We should of course oppose it. Neither should we uphold houses of ill fame. It goes without saying that we must do all in our power to stamp them out. And it is our sacred duty to bend our every effort toward making the world a decent place to live in. We *did* give our money and our sons for this cause. Yet we repeat: the devil would not mind if all the efforts of men in the directions just indicated should be crowned with success. Do you wonder what we are driving at? We answer that nothing could aid him more in keeping men away from the cross of Christ, in forcing to the background the gospel of the crucified Christ. Men would rely upon their own righteousness instead of Christ's. Human righteousness would be substituted for divine. Men would imagine themselves so good that they would not need to be washed in the blood of the Lamb.

To that, we take it, Paul referred when he wrote to the church at Corinth: 'And no marvel; for Satan himself is transformed into an angel of light. Therefore it is no great thing if his ministers also be transformed as the *ministers of righteousness*' (*2 Cor.* 11:14).

Just one more point we wish to make. It can be stated very briefly. The Bible tells us that in a supernatural way God will provide for the continuance of his church on earth. 'Not by might, nor by power, but by my Spirit, saith the Lord of hosts' (*Zech.* 4:6). The Spirit of God will take care of the church. But the up-to-date church, instead of relying upon God for prosperity, enlists the aid of all kinds of human inventions. By special music, big orators, and curious subjects the audience is drawn. And the institutional church seeks to maintain itself by such attractions as a swimming pool, a gymnasium, a lunch-counter, and mayhap a dance-hall. Surely, that is a denial of the supernatural.

We are now ready to draw a conclusion:

The church is a supernatural institution. But the church is itself denying the supernatural. Think of it: a supernatural institution flouting the supernatural! What does it mean but that the church is digging its own grave? And now do you marvel that people are leaving the church, that in many cases churches with seating capacity for a thousand are attended by some fifty? Nothing could be more natural. In the supernatural lies the church's reason for existence. Now if the supernatural is ruled out, the church loses its reason for existence. The sooner its doors are closed, the better. So men reason, and they are right. Jesus reasons the same way. Says he to the church: 'I will spue thee out of my mouth' (*Rev.* 3:16).

If the Saviour should come today, would he find faith on the earth? Precious little!

That the church's departure from the faith is a sign of Jesus' coming is perfectly plain. God tells us so in several places besides our text. Throughout the New Testament it is taught that the Saviour's advent will be preceded by a great apostasy. Now the question remains to be answered, *why* Jesus is going to appear just then when the church is so very decadent. The complete answer we cannot hope to give. We mention only two reasons.

Believers are the salt of the earth. Our text tells us that the salt will lose its savour. Consequently the earth will be practically saltless. And that means that God will no longer taste of it. He will assign it to the dunghill, to the garbage-dump, to the valley of the son of Hinnom. Judgment day will come.

The church is the body of Christ on earth. In the latter days so little faith will be left that Christ's body will seem to have perished from the earth. The prince of lies will seem to have gained a complete victory over the church as piIlar and mainstay of the truth.

Just then the Christ will interfere to save his body, to preserve the truth, to turn seeming defeat into glorious victory.

To us comes the command to contend earnestly for the faith once delivered to the saints. We behold Jesus arising from the right hand of the Father and preparing to step into the cloud. As he does so, he calls out to us: 'Thou hast a little strength, and hast kept my word, and hast not denied my name ... Behold, I come quickly; hold fast that which thou hast, that no man take thy crown' (*Rev.* 3:8, 11)!

4

The Missionary Age

And this gospel of the kingdom shall be preached in
all the world for a witness unto all nations;
and then shall the end come.

MATTHEW 24:14

DAY IS WONT TO DAWN GRADUALLY. Surely, yet slowly, at a given moment imperceptibly, light replaces darkness. It cannot be said with accuracy what time the stars fade from vision, what time any one star vanishes. They melt away. Whatever clouds chance to hang in the eastern sky pass through a hundred shades of blue and red and yellow. Rays of golden light herald sunrise.

How differently the day of God will break! It will not dawn. With the suddenness of a flash of lightning will it burst upon the earth. In the twinkling of an eye blackest darkness will be replaced by brightest light.

There will also be *resemblance*. Just before the appearance of the first signs of dawn the night's darkness is said to be deepest. So too the bursting of God's day will be preceded by awful darkness. From the Christian viewpoint, conditions on earth will be dreadful, the plight of the church will be deplorable. In their thoughts the serious-minded will involuntarily draw a comparison between their own times and the exceedingly dark days before the flood. It will seem that the world is going to hell. So black will its darkness be that it will become increasingly difficult to distinguish earth from hell.

No wonder that many, nay most, of the signs of the coming of the Son of man are sad, unfavourable, lamentable. The picture which God has painted in his Word of the days preceding judgment is very dark. Yet, thanks to the divine grace, both common and particular, the picture is not perfectly black. Earth will never be hell. At least a few signs of Jesus' coming are favourable.

This time we wish to preach on a very prominent favourable sign of the times. We are thinking of the wonderful missionary activity of the church of Christ in our day, an activity so great that our age deserves to be designated as THE MISSIONARY AGE. With that in mind, let us turn to the study of our text.

Jesus tells us that the end will come when the gospel of the kingdom shall have been preached in all the world for a witness unto all nations. We call to your attention that *this prophecy* —

a.   *Is sometimes misunderstood .*

b.   *Is wonderfully being fulfilled.*

c.   *Is powerfully stimulating.*

d.   *Is rapidly nearing final fulfilment.*

a. Our text does not tell us that the gospel will be preached to *every individual,* but that it will reach *all nations.* Here is a distinction which some lose sight of. The result is that they fall into grievous error.

If the end were not coming until the gospel has been preached to all *individuals,* the chances are that it would be quite distant. There are millions of individuals here in Christian lands – not to speak of the heathen – who have never had the gospel preached to them, .who never heard the blessed name of Jesus used except in a curse. But now that the end will come as soon as all *nations* have been reached by the gospel, it may be very near.

We must call attention to a point of difference between the Methodist way of carrying on missionary work and the Reformed method. Methodist missionaries think, surely not exclusively, yet generally, in terms of individuals. That is why they talk so much about the value of a single soul. That is also the reason why they like to count the number of their converts. Reformed missionaries are just as anxious that individuals be saved. They attach at least as much value to the individual soul. But they usually look farther than do their Methodist brethren. They take a broader view of the matter. So wide is their vision that it includes whole nations. They think, more than their Wesleyan co-labourers, in terms of nations. Our text also speaks in terms of nations. So we may say that our text is Reformed; or better, that the Reformed way of viewing missionary work is biblical.

Some people think that all nations will have to be converted, actually Christianized, before the end can come. That view is held by the so-called Postmillenarians. It seems to them that the world is gradually getting better, that humanity is becoming more Christlike. Especially through the church's missionary efforts will the world's moral and religious progress be enhanced, say they. After a while all nations will be Christian. Then we shall have the golden age, the millennium, a thousand years of undisturbed peace. At the close of the thousand years the forces of evil will be let loose. They will have free play, but only for a short season. Suddenly the Christ will come and plant his heel upon his foe's neck.

That Jesus teaches nothing of the kind is perfectly plain. He does not say that all nations will *be converted,* just that they will *hear the gospel.* He even adds that the gospel will be preached *as a witness* unto all nations, and that implies that not all will accept the message. So our text teaches quite the opposite of Postmillennialism. And then, how anybody can still hold to such a view in these days when the Christian nations have just been pitted against each other, nay, have held on to one another with bulldog grip for more than four years in the bloodiest war of all history, is far more than we can understand. It seems that men would finally wake up to the fact that all this talk about the world's getting better, about the present ushering in of a golden age in which all the nations will be Christian, is sheer tommy-rot. Let us rejoice that we shall not have to wait for Christ's return until that has come to pass.

Bear in mind a distinction. The *Christianizing* of the world and the *evangelizing* of the world are not the same. Christianized the world never will be in this dispensation. Evangelized the world will have to be before the Saviour can return. And of evangelizing Jesus speaks. The gospel, the evangel, will be preached in the whole world as a witness unto all nations.

Does it follow that, as we carry the gospel to the nations, we should not at all be concerned as to whether they accept it? Does it follow, since all nations never will be Christianized, that we need not *try* to Christianize them? Most emphatically not. Just before his ascent to heaven, the Master told the apostles not merely to evangelize the nations, but literally *to make disciples* of them all (*Matt.* 28:19). So warm, so spirited should be our gospel message as though there were every prospect of bringing all nations on their knees before God's Christ. And if you ask what is the use of Christ's commanding the impossible and of our attempting it, then we answer that it is of the very essence of Christianity to reach out for unattainable ideals. Do Christians not run with all their might toward the goal of perfection, though they know that they will not attain it in this life? Do not Christians pray, 'Thy will be done in earth, as it is in heaven', though they are aware that the present dispensation will not bring the fulfilment of this petition? So too they attempt to disciple all nations, though it has been revealed to them that, when Jesus comes, the nations will only be evangelized.

An important question suggests itself. Why must Christ's return wait for the evangelizing of the world? Why cannot Christ come back until the gospel has been preached to all peoples?

An answer frequently given is that God desires to give all nations a chance to turn to him, in order that, on the day of judgment, not a single nation may be able to say, 'I knew not the way, therefore I failed to walk in it'; in a word, in order that, on the great day of accounting, all nations may be without excuse. Maybe that reply does not look very good to you. You say, 'Men will be judged not as nations but as individuals. To me it seems that every individual ought to receive a chance to accept the gospel.' We remind you that many Christians think the Word teaches that there is going to be not merely a judgment of individuals, but also a separate judgment of nations. But even if you do not agree to this, yet the above answer can stand. It should always be remembered that God takes into account, much more than we are wont to, the organic relation of men to men. The covenant idea, of which we of the Reformed faith make so much, is based upon this fact. God regards the human race not merely as so many individuals, but rather as so many families, as so many tribes, as so many peoples. God deals with men not merely as individuals, but very often as organic groups of individuals. That is an important truth which we are apt to forget in our extremely individualistic age. And so it is God's concern to give each nation the opportunity to receive the gospel. If the opportunity is not grasped, no excuse will be left on judgment day. How plainly that is implied in the words of our text that the gospel will be preached to all nations *for a witness*.

Then too, is it not true that in the nation's opportunity lies that of the individual? That surely holds of the individuals in a nation who are living at the time when the light of the gospel shines upon their people. Think, for instance, of our own American people. To be sure, there are millions of men and women and children in our land with little more knowledge of the gospel of Jesus Christ than is found among the natives of the darkest parts of the dark continent. But have they not the chance to make the gospel's acquaintance? Do not the majority of them live within walking distance of a Christian church? Cannot all of them buy the Word of God for a few pennies?

There is another reason why Jesus cannot come until all nations have heard the gospel. It is a beautiful one. God's love embraces *the world*. 'For God so loved *the world*, that he gave his only begotten Son, that whosoever believeth in him should not perish, but have everlasting life' (*John* 3:16). Among other things this means that God has his elect in all nations, not a single one excepted. From East to West, from pole to pole, those objects of the divine love live scattered. That is why God wants the gospel to be preached in all the world. Only thus will all the elect be gathered in. And so the song of the redeemed in glory becomes possible: 'Thou [O Lamb] wast slain, and hast redeemed us to God by thy blood out of every kindred and tongue and people and nation' (*Rev.* 5:9).

b. They were dark days for the gospel of the kingdom when Jesus spoke these words. As yet it had been preached only in the little land of the Jews, a speck on the map. *The* Preacher of the gospel, Jesus himself, had met with so little success that the number of his followers seemed negligible. Worse than that, he was in daily danger of losing his life at the hands of his enemies. It must have seemed to the disciples, when Jesus spoke of evangelizing the world, that the Master was such a dreamer, so extreme a visionary, that he no longer listened to the voice of common sense. The days continued dark for some time to come. Before his ascension the Lord commanded his followers to preach the gospel to all nations. They set out to do so. But hardly had they begun when some of them were cast into prison, others killed, and the rest scattered to the four winds. Ah, in their prayers they must oft have sighed, 'Lord, what of thy prophecy that the whole world is to be evangelized?'

'Wonderful in counsel, and excellent in working' is the Lord God (*Isa.* 28:29). Mark! When the evangelization of the world seemed hopeless, it was progressing most beautifully. When the powers of the world resolved to crush the gospel, it burst forth irresistibly. For each gospel banner torn down a hundred new ones arose. The early Christians were scattered this way and that by persecution. But exactly these scattered Christians had unexcelled opportunity to cast the gospel seed abroad. So they did. The seed sprouted. The tidings of salvation were well off on their triumphal march around the globe.

Just as wonderfully, perhaps even more wonderfully, is God seeing to the fulfilment of the prophecy of our text today.

The church is on the decline. The decline is as sad as rapid. It is extremely rapid. The truth is being cast overboard. Heresies not only abound outside the church, but are proclaimed as unquestionable truth by its leaders within. One would almost question whether the church may still be called 'pillar and stay of the truth'. But now observe a wonderful phenomenon! This decadent church is putting forth such mighty missionary efforts as the world has never before witnessed. *This age of the church's decline is at the same time the age of missions.*

When we enquire – and we cannot help enquiring – how that is possible, the case becomes even more wonderful. Listen! *It is a fact that the very decadence of the church is helping along the cause of missions.*

Let us adduce some proof for that almost unbelievable statement.

One of the most outstanding features of present-day Christianity is its extreme practicalism. Especially does that hold of

American Christianity, which is ruled by the spirit of Methodism. Theory and practice, doctrine and life, theology and Christian work are arrayed over against each other. Theory, doctrine, and theology are scorned. Practice, life, and Christian work are eulogized. It matters little what a man believes so long as he is active, doing the King's business. That is the utterly foolish talk which you hear everywhere today. And a threefold woe is pronounced over the head of him who indulges in theological strife while the heathen are perishing.

This attitude is doing the Christian church untold harm. It is causing it to drift from the purity of doctrine and therefore to lose its only sure moorings. And yet it must be granted that this very spirit of extreme practicalism is responsible for a large portion of contemporary missionary activity. In fact it would seem that the most Methodistically inclined churches are most active for the cause of missions.

Another outstanding characteristic of the Christian church of our day – one very closely related to that just mentioned – is what, may be called the fading away of boundary lines. All of us know that, for several decades already, there has existed a strong movement to unite all Christian churches, both Protestant and Roman Catholic. Now it must be granted that the unity of the church of Christ is a grand ideal which we too may well keep before our mind's eye. At the same time it may never be forgotten that this ideal will not be realized until Christ returns. And especially would we emphasize this: our great objection to present-day efforts to realize this ideal is that they would compel the purer churches to sacrifice some of their purity, which, of course, they may never consent to. Small wonder that the so-called liberals are the hardest workers for the cause. But to them we refuse to listen. And yet who can deny that this tendency toward church-union has been productive of great results in the field of missions? *In unity there is strength*. Such gatherings as the World Missionary Conferences exert no small power. 'The harmony displayed at these conferences gives the impression that Protestant foreign missionaries should be considered a single force, and that they stand in the foremost' rank of powers destined to change the face of the world' (W. D. MacKenzie).

In the third place, we refer to the humanitarian – or shall we say: humanistic? – spirit that is sweeping the churches. The Universal Fatherhood of God and the Universal Brotherhood of Man seem to have become the church's most fundamental doctrines. All men are brethren. The heathen also are our brethren. Therefore, so we are told, it is our duty to bring them the gospel. It would be cruel for us to delay. Now that reasoning seems very superficial to him who stands squarely on Reformed truth. He at once detects the blunder which we heard an instructor at one of our State Universities point out a few years ago. Said he: 'Christians today are emphasizing the second table of the law at the expense of the first.' Even more, he realizes that the Universal Fatherhood of God and the Universal Brotherhood of Man have become extremely misleading terms. And yet it cannot be gainsaid that humanitarian motives account for a great deal of giving for missions: giving of money, and giving of selves.

The church's externalism ought to receive at least passing attention. The church wants to be big, outwardly big. Big congregations, big buildings, big offerings; big statistics; these are some of the things which the church is driving at. Now it is all wrong to press these matters into the foreground. It is decidedly unchristian. How can it be harmonized with Jesus' statement, 'The kingdom of God cometh not with observation' (*Luke* 17:20)? And yet, in line with this desire for bigness is the demand for big missionary forces in big fields at big distances from home to do big things for God.

Finally we call attention to materialism in the church. Some of us have read Winston Churchill's[1] *The Inside of the Cup*. This book contains much falsehood. It is just full of the worst kind of poison. But it brings out forcibly the important truth that there are lots of men in the Christian church today who have become wealthy through fraudulent practices, and now try to ease their consciences by giving of their tainted money liberally to such noble causes as Christian missions. And is it not true that love of money has pervaded the people of our land; also, generally speaking, the membership of its churches? And can it be denied that just because there is so much money in the church, the church has been able to increase its missionary efforts tenfold?

Now do not misunderstand! It is by no means our contention that *all* or *almost all* of the church's missionary activity in our day must be accounted for by the church's decadence. God forbid that we should say anything of the kind! There are many more than seven thousand in the church whose motive is obedience to the Master's great command. Yet we repeat: *the very decadence of the church is helping along the cause of missions.*

'O the depth of the riches both of the wisdom and knowledge of God! how unsearchable are his judgments, and his ways past finding out!' (*Rom.* 11:33).

c. What encouragement our text contains! The gospel *will* be preached to all nations. The time is coming that every nation will be acquainted with the only name given under heaven among men by which they can be saved. All the powers of the world, all the demons of hell, cannot prevent it.

Even better, *this gospel of the kingdom* will be proclaimed in all the world. Many so-called missionaries of the cross do not

---

[1] A best-selling American novelist (1871–1947), not to be confused with Sir Winston Churchill (1874–1965), the British statesman and wartime leader.

deserve their name. They are messengers of the prince of lies rather than of the God of all truth. Quite a number preach civilization instead of regeneration, reform instead of repentance, salvation by works instead of by grace. It might be doubted whether the true gospel will reach all nations. Yet there is no cause for worry. Jesus gives the assurance-that *this gospel of the kingdom* will be preached everywhere, and he means the very same gospel which he has been proclaiming. And is it not a remarkable fact that, in spite of the departure from the faith found among missionaries, yet, generally speaking, the preachers of the gospel in heathen lands excel those in Christian lands in point of orthodoxy? The old-time gospel is heard more frequently from missionaries abroad than from ministers at home.

Surely, our text is full of encouragement. To Christianize the world may be impossible. Our task to evangelize the world lies well within the bounds of possibility. It *can* be done. Then why be discouraged? It *will* be accomplished. Onward then, Christian soldiers! Victory is in sight!

The very fact that the world can be evangelized and will be, should act as a powerful stimulant for us in our missionary efforts. But Jesus administers an even more powerful stimulant.

All Christians long for the coming of their Lord. They pray very often: 'Thy Kingdom come!' Every once in a while they pray: 'Come, Lord Jesus, yea, come quickly!' Who in *these* days does not utter that prayer every day? There is no more fervent desire in the Christian's heart than that Jesus may come back soon. If he is the right kind of Christian, that desire almost consumes him. But now observe! Jesus will not come back until the world has been evangelized. From the right hand of the Father he is watching us in our attempts to evangelize the nations. He is waiting for us to complete our task. So long as we are not through, he cannot come. But when we are through, then presently, immediately, all of a sudden, he will appear. So if we are slothful about preaching the gospel we are delaying Christ's return. But who would be guilty of that? And the more energetic, the more zealous, the more fiery, the more spirited we are about our work, the sooner he will come.

Then will you not give your time, your money, your son, your daughter, your life, for missions?

d. About how much longer before we may expect the gospel to have finished its crusade around the globe? In other words, about how much longer before we may expect Jesus to return? If we answered that question with an attempt at definiteness, we would be doing what we said at the beginning of this series we would not do. It would amount to an attempt to satisfy your curiosity. We shall not be so foolish as to make any kind of a guess at the length of time separating us from the end. What we must do however, is to point out that the prophecy of our text is rapidly nearing its final fulfilment.

Will you pardon a brief personal reference? Some ten years ago we had the privilege of representing the students of our Christian Reformed Seminary at the Rochester Convention of the Student Volunteer Movement. Already at that time the ideal was held up before us of evangelizing the world 'in this generation'. A generation is usually figured at about thirty years. Nor was that ideal the outcome of wild enthusiasm. It was based upon the findings of some of the world's foremost missionary authorities.

Our age is *the* age of missions *par excellence.* Everybody knows that. Nobody questions it. To prove it with statistics is needless. We give just a few figures suggestive of the tremendous zeal with which the Christian church is pushing missionary efforts. The Protestant churches of North America are said to have given $19,600,000 for foreign missions last year. Think of it: during

1918, when the war demanded so many billions of dollars! The number of baptized Christians in India has increased at the rate of more than 10,000 a month during the last five years. Just think: more than 600,000 of the people of India baptized in the name of the Triune God in only five years!

Statistics tell us that the world contains many more heathen than Christians at the present time. That would seem to indicate that the complete evangelization of the world is still a long way off. But the conclusion is not warranted. Several nations which have already been pretty thoroughly evangelized still contain large numbers of heathen. Japan is a rather striking example. And it must not be forgotten that whole lands which once enjoyed the light of the gospel have fallen back into the darkness of paganism or are now in the clutches of Mohammedanism. Asia Minor and Northern Africa are examples. These lands have had their day. They cannot expect another opportunity.

When Jesus spoke to his disciples about *the whole world*, they thought of the Roman world. That was practically all of the world that was known at the time. And it was evangelized rather soon. For our forefathers of the fifteenth century the world was considerably larger, yet it was still comparatively small. They knew nothing about America. So the world has been growing. Ever have new lands, new continents, been discovered. The world ever proved bigger than men thought it was. And as it kept growing, the fulfilment of Jesus' prophecy was delayed. But now the world is growing no more. It is reasonably certain that no new lands of any considerable extent will be discovered. When the world as we know it today shall have been evangelized, then the end will come.

The world is no longer growing larger, we said. We might have said that it is growing smaller. Our age is one of commerce. Commerce necessitates the laying of trans-continental railroads, the building of vessels that plough the oceans. Thus commerce draws nations together. And in that way it aids tremendously to hasten the evangelization of the world, to hasten the end.

What effect has the war had and will it have on missions? Many fear that the war will prove a serious setback to the cause. Is that likely? This question deserves serious, albeit brief, consideration. The distinction between Christianizing and evangelizing will again aid us much as we attempt to find the correct answer.

It can hardly be questioned that the war has done irreparable damage to the Christianizing of the pagan and Mohammedan nations. The awful conflict of Christian nation against Christian nation has caused their respect for the Christian religion to diminish. Missionaries tell us that this is sadly noticeable. What else could be expected?

But how about the evangelization of the world? In a way the war has injured also this cause. Two thousand German missionaries are said to have been called or driven out of Africa in the course of the war. Several missionaries and candidates for the work were slain in battle. Most of the great Protestant nations were crippled financially. All that is very deplorable. Yet almost all of these setbacks may be considered temporary. In a few years these matters can be re-adjusted. And over against them stand certain great advantages that are bound to accrue from the war for the evangelization of the nations. The methods of raising war-money employed so successfully by the governments, have taught the churches a lesson. Mighty campaigns for raising missionary funds are being set on foot. In our own country there is the Inter-Church Movement, which proposes to obtain two hundred millions of dollars for missionary, educational, and benevolent purposes each year beginning in 1920. More important than this, the power of Turkey, the political backbone of Mohammedanism, that powerful rival of Christianity in Asia and Africa, has been broken. Most important of all the war has been a very powerful agent in bringing nations together which formerly stood far apart. Heathen and Mohammedan nations were brought into the closest kind of contact with Christian nations. Inevitably the former are going to make the acquaintance of the gospel.

We may safely conclude that, though the war likely did great and lasting harm to the cause of the world's Christianization, it will eventually prove to have furthered the cause of the nations' evangelization considerably.

Once more, ours is *the missionary age.* Tremendous, stupendous, unprecedented in the history of Christianity, are the missionary efforts put forth by the church of Christ today. Ours is also *the age of the church's departure from the faith,* With extreme rapidity is the church deteriorating spiritually. When we attempt to put these two facts together, we marvel. The thing is wonderful in our eyes.

We see the hand of God. We exclaim: Behold a sign of the times! Our hearts begin to throb with joy. Our souls are consumed with longing. We lift our faces upward. Our eyes attempt to pierce the clouds. We strain our ears to catch the welcome sound of angels' trumpets.

5

Present-Day Antichrists

For many shall come in my name, saying,
I am Christ; and shall deceive many.

MATTHEW 24:5

Little children, it is the last time: and as ye have heard that
antichrist shall come, even now are there many antichrists;
whereby we know that it is the last time.

1 JOHN 2:18

*T*HE *ANTICHRIST* – there you have a subject on which certain
Christians like to speculate. Some go wild about it, as is shown
by the absurd opinion which made considerable headway
during the war, that Kaiser Wilhelm II of Germany would prove
to be the Antichrist.

We shall approach the subject in a calm, deliberate way. And
so, first of all, we wish to explain the name *Antichrist. Anti* may
mean *against. Anti* may also mean *instead of.* In this particular case
it has both meanings. So the Antichrist will be against the Christ;
he will be the Christ's great opponent. He will also be in Christ's
stead; that is to say, he will be an imitation of the Christ, a counterfeit Christ. *A counterfeit Christ, the mighty opponent of the true
Christ, the devil's imitation of God's Christ – that* is our definition of
the Antichrist. In following this sermon, you do well to bear that
definition in mind.

The Antichrist will be some one person, a single individual, who is to make his appearance just before Christ's return. But please observe! As the real Christ was prefigured by several Biblical persons, so was also the Antichrist. We mention but a few names. Abel, Moses, David, and Solomon were types of the Christ. Cain, Pharaoh, Saul, and Jeroboam were types of the Antichrist.

The Christ *has* come into the world. He came more than nineteen centuries ago. And then his types were fulfilled. But the Antichrist has not yet put in his appearance. His types are not yet fulfilled. To the contrary, they are being multiplied. New ones are ever presenting themselves. Ever and anon the Antichrist is being prefigured in new ways.

Antiochus Epiphanes, the cruel oppressor of God's ancient people, was a striking type of the Antichrist. So was the Roman emperor Nero, that monster, who is said to have beheaded the chief of the apostles of the Christ, and, while he feasted in his gardens, to have lighted them with human torches, the pitch-and-tar-covered bodies of Christians. The apostle John saw Antichrist typified in several heretics of his day. He refers to them in our text. And so every succeeding age has had its types of the Antichrist, and every age to come will have them, until Satan's counterpart of God's Christ actually makes his appearance. Our age too has its Antichrists.

At this point we wish to make an announcement that may disappoint a few in the audience. Maybe you are in hopes of hearing a sermon on the Antichrist. You would like to hear us – or, for that matter, any other preacher – speculate on this subject. But you are not going to. A sermon on *the* Antichrist would hardly fit into this series on the signs of the times. By *signs of the times* we mean *present* conditions, *present* events, which surely point to the future, but nevertheless lie in *the present. In this whole series of sermons we are concerned not so much with the future as with the present.* But the

Antichrist is not yet present among us. He is coming. He may come soon, very soon in fact. But we cannot now raise our index-finger and cry out: Behold, the Antichrist!

Our subject is not: the Antichrist. It is: PRESENT-DAY ANTI-CHRISTS.

We cannot in a single sermon discuss all present-day Antichrists. If we attempted it, we should have to touch on nearly every heresy of our times. And their number is almost as the stars of heaven. So we are compelled to make a selection. It seems best to choose certain prominent heresies that call themselves by the name of Christ; that boldly claim to be Christian; to which the words of Jesus apply very evidently: 'Many shall come in my name, saying, I am Christ.'

We call attention to four of them. They are

a. Romanism.
b. Christian Science.
c. Christian Socialism.
d. The very widespread teaching of the Divinity of Man.

a. There was a time when Protestants generally had their minds made up that the pope was the Antichrist. A Lutheran calling this into question could be a member of the Lutheran church no more. And to the question, 'Who is Antichrist?', the Reformed catechism books answered in the most matter-of-fact way, 'The Romish Pope.'

Today most Protestants smile about the idea that the pope is Antichrist. They think it ridiculous. 'Our forefathers came to that conclusion', they say, 'or rather jumped at it, in the heat of their strife with Rome. We have cooled off; we take a saner view of the matter. To us it is plain as broad daylight that the pope is not Antichrist.'

We hold that our hot-headed fathers were more nearly right than their cold-blooded, easy-going, pussy-footed, milk-and-water children. Though the pope is assuredly not *the* Antichrist, yet he is *an* Antichrist. That proposition we hope to prove.

That Romanism comes in the name of Christ is so generally known that it may almost be considered waste of time to point this out.

The Romish church calls itself the *Catholic* Church. It claims to contain all the believers. There are no true believers outside the church. Salvation cannot be obtained outside of it. All of which amounts to the boast that the Romish church is *the* Christian church, *the body of Christ on earth.* Says Rome in proud conceit, *'Christ's body am I.'*

How prominent a place the Christ occupies in the very architecture of a Romish church building! Already at a distance you behold the gilded cross on a high spire glittering in the unobstructed rays of the sun. The two side-walls of the interior are decorated with the stations of the cross, so-called, representing various events which occurred, or are supposed to have occurred, as the cross-laden Jesus travelled the heavy road from Jerusalem to Calvary. In the place of greatest prominence stands the altar, on which the Christ is wont to be sacrificed anew at every celebration of the mass. And no matter to which nook or corner you turn, your gaze is arrested by a crucifix on which hangs the blood-stained figure of the Saviour.

The life of Christ on earth was full of miracles. Rome also claims to perform miracles. Thousands of invalids make a pilgrimage annually to the fountains of the city of Lourdes in France. Some years as many as 300,000 are said to go. From time to time the Virgin Mary is reported to appear, and to trouble the waters. And those who are so fortunate as to enter the water or to catch a glimpse of the Virgin's benign face are healed of their diseases.

The blood of the prophets, the teeth of the apostles, the bones of the saints, and the hair of the martyrs are carefully preserved in the churches; and these relics too are said to have effected wonderful cures.

Bolder than that: the pope, the head of Romanism, is designated the *vicar of Christ*. Christ himself having gone to heaven, he has appointed the pope to take his place on earth. He speaks with authority as did the Christ, nay, even infallibly. In the Name of the Son of God he forgives sins.

Add to all this the fact, which is extremely humiliating for us Protestants, that, while Protestantism is undermining the authority of the Bible, Romanism is coming forward as the champion defender of Holy Writ as the Word of God; and, while Protestantism is desecrating holy matrimony, Romanism is holding high the sanctity of the marriage-tie. Surely, it must be granted that beyond the shadow of a doubt Romanism comes in the name of Christ, saying, 'I am Christ.'

But is it not just as evident that Romanism comes *falsely* in the name of Christ, that it is a counterfeit Christ, an Antichrist? Just listen.

The Jews have rejected Jesus as the Christ. For that reason they deny that the Old Testament ceremonies have found their fulfilment. So far as possible, they keep these ceremonies as did their fathers in the days of Moses and of Solomon. But is not Romanism just interwoven with Judaisms? They may be seen everywhere on the surface. Is not the Romish priesthood sufficient evidence? Romanism like Judaism, Romanism by its Judaisms, denies Jesus the Christ.

Romanism abounds with paganisms. It teaches its followers to kneel before images of wood or stone, as do the heathen. Pagan festivals, the feast-days of pagan Rome, it has adopted for its own, changing only their outer garb. And do you not recall what the

Heidelberg Catechism says so fearlessly and faultlessly about the Romish mass? It calls it 'accursed idolatry' (Question 80).

Jesus said, 'Him that cometh to me I will in no wise cast out' (*John* 6:37). Romanism says that no man may come to the Saviour directly; that he can be approached only through an intercessor, as Mary, for instance.

Jesus said, 'Search the Scriptures' (*John* 5:39). Romanism regards Scripture-reading as dangerous for the ordinary layman.

Jesus said, 'All they that take the sword shall perish with the sword' (*Matt.* 26:52). Romanism has relied on the sword for extending the papal domain. On the never-to-be-forgotten night of St Bartholomew, 24 August 1572, Romanism slew as many as eight thousand faithful followers of the Christ with the sword.

Jesus said, 'My kingdom is not of this world' (*John* 18:36). Romanism has long enjoyed great worldly power, and is seeking slyly yet eagerly to regain it. Romanism would like once more to control the politics of the world. And here you have a very evident mark of the Antichrist. The teaching of Scripture is plain that the Antichrist will wield unlimited *political* power.

On the great feast-days of the Romish church the 'Holy Father' is wont to be carried into St Peter's on the shoulders of men, placed on the high altar, and there to all intents and purposes worshipped. Does that not make you think at once of Paul's description of the Antichrist, in which he tells us that he will sit as God in the temple of God, showing himself that he is God (*2 Thess.* 2:4)?

Would you know how squarely Romanism is opposed to the Christ? Then read John's striking description of her in the seventeenth chapter of Revelation. He pictures her as a woman seated upon a scarlet beast with seven heads and ten horns. She is decked with gold and precious stones and pearls. Her name is the mother of harlots. She is drunk with the blood of the saints.

We are very much afraid that there is a tendency among Protestants nowadays to minimize the Romish peril. The (in certain respects) very tolerant spirit of our age has helped much to create this tendency. Such violent anti-Romish propaganda as is made, for instance, by *The Menace* has served to strengthen it. That kind of propaganda overreaches the mark. We naturally recoil from it. And some of our Reformed people of Holland descent have become almost sympathetic toward Romanism under influences coming, strange to say, from the old country, where in Reformation days the conflict between Romanism and Protestantism was so extremely bitter. Of late the Reformed and the Romanists have frequently co-operated politically in the Netherlands.

But it is dangerous to underestimate the Romish peril. Just let us give you some idea of the progress of Romanism in the last century. A little more than a hundred years ago England had but thirty-three Romish priests. Today it has some twenty-five thousands. And as for our own United States, while the population has increased twenty-five times in a hundred years, the Romish population has increased three hundred and twenty times.

The war has aided the cause of Romanism. More correctly put, Romanism grasped the opportunity offered by the war to push its cause. The Knights of Columbus exerted a mighty influence on almost all the men in service. How highly the soldiers and sailors speak of this organization! It ought to have credit for all the good work it did. But is it not deplorable that many of the men returning home from service have practically lost sight of the line of demarcation between Romanism and Protestantism?

b. Christian Science comes in the name of Christ, saying, 'I am Christ.' That is true most literally. Just listen to the claims put forth for it by its founder, Mrs Mary Baker Eddy. Says she, 'Christ is simply a spiritual idea. Christian Science is that idea.' Again she says, 'The coming of Christian Science is the second coming of Christ.' We ask: can you imagine a more literal fulfilment of the Saviour's prophecy, 'Many will come in my name, saying, I am Christ'? Christian Science says point blank, 'I am Christ.' Have you ever passed by the Christian Science temple on Washington Street in our city? If you have, your first impression must have been that you had a Christian church before you. In bold relief on the exterior walls are written the words of Jesus, 'Preach the gospel. Heal the sick.' Yes, Christian Science comes in the name of Christ.

Christ performed miracles. Christian Science claims to perform miracles. Hers are of exactly the same kind as were his. The sick are healed in wonderful ways.

That Christian Science comes in the name of Christ is self-evident. We shall waste no words on that point. At greater length we desire to make plain that it comes *falsely* in the name of Christ; that it is a counterfeit Christ, an Antichrist.

The very fact that Christian Science claims to perform miracles casts upon it the suspicion of unreliability. Did not Jesus foretell just that kind of thing? He said: 'For false Christs and false prophets shall rise, and *shall show signs and wonders,* to seduce, if it were possible, even the elect' (*Mark* 13:22).

One of the fundamentals of Christian Science is the denial of matter. Matter is said not to exist. The things that we see, smell, hear, taste, and touch, we do not in reality see, smell, hear, taste, and touch. We only imagine it. From, this it follows at once that no man was ever born, and of course also that Jesus Christ never came in the flesh. Christian Science proclaims that without the least hesitation. How evident a mark of the Antichrist! Says John in his first epistle, 'Hereby know ye the Spirit of God: Every spirit that confesseth that Jesus Christ is come in the flesh is of God: and every spirit that confesseth not that Jesus Christ is come in the flesh is not of God: and this is that spirit of Antichrist, whereof ye have heard that it should come; and even now already is it in the world' (*1 John* 4:2,3). And in his second letter he repeats, 'For many deceivers are entered into the world, who confess not that Jesus Christ is come in the flesh. This is a deceiver and an antichrist' (*2 John* 7).

Another fundamental of Christian Science is the denial of sin. Sin simply does not exist, we are told. The sooner we get rid of the error that there is sin, the purer and the holier we shall be. Now if that be true, then we surely need no Saviour from sin. Thus the Christ of Scripture is cast headlong overboard.

Now if we put these two fundamentals together: the denial of matter and the denial of sin, mark to what conclusion we are driven! Because there is no sin, Jesus *did not have to* shed his blood on Calvary. Because there is no matter, there is no such thing as blood; consequently, Jesus *did not* shed his blood on Calvary. The sacrificial death of Christ is ruled out. *Thus Christian Science, though calling itself Christian, plucks the very heart out of Christianity.*

What does Christian Science say about the Bible? It calls it a fallible book, a book full of error. And therefore it is not safe to read it except when Mrs Eddy's infallible book, *Science and Health*, is used as a guide. Have you ever heard greater blasphemy? *God's Word is said to be fallible; Mrs Eddy's infallible.*

When Jesus was on earth, he was worse off than the foxes and the birds. They had holes and nests. But he, the Son of man, had no place to rest his weary head. Now mark the contrast! Such was the founder of Christianity. But the founder of Christian Science was one of the wealthiest women in all of rich America. She spent her days in luxury.

During his stay on earth, Jesus laboured among the poor and the despised. Ignorant Galilean fishermen became his associates.

Publicans with the smell of liquor on their breath were his friends. But Christian Science has almost all of its adherents among the rich, the so-called cultured, the men and women – especially the latter – of high society. Do you get the contrast?

Christianity tells women to refrain from teaching in the assembly of the saints. Christian Science was founded by a woman. And the case of this woman bears a striking resemblance to that of mother Eve. Some one has aptly said, 'The devil fooled the world through the first woman; he is now trying to fool the world through another woman. He led it into sin through the first woman; he would lead it away from the remedy of sin through the other woman' (Haldeman).

Does not the very name Christian *Science* remind you of Paul's admonition to Timothy, 'O Timothy, keep that which is committed to thy trust, avoiding profane and vain babblings, and oppositions of *science falsely so called'* (*1 Tim.* 6:20)?

Surely we do not go a bit too far when we call Christian Science the Judas Iscariot of Christianity. Coming in the name of Christ, it betrays Christianity to the devil.

c. Christian Socialism demands our attention. We all know in a general way what is meant by Socialism. Let us state briefly what is meant by *Christian* Socialism.

It has many adherents among Christian ministers. They talk roughly as follows: The church has been speaking altogether too much to men, especially to the poor, about the joys awaiting them on yonder side the grave. It is more than time that we forget about these hazy speculations and, to come right down to brass tacks, seek to make men happy here and now. Let us stop talking about spiritual food; let us give the working man a full dinner-pail. Let us stop picturing a golden city above the clouds; let us have sanitary cities studded with parks and playgrounds here below. Let us stop prating about the Father's house with its many mansions; rather let us see to it that every family gets a cosy home on earth, with a flower-bed in front, a lawn on either side, and a vegetable garden in the rear.

In a word, let us stop preaching about the invisible, and restrict ourselves to the visible; let us lay all emphasis on this side the grave instead of yonder side. Let us shift the emphasis from individual salvation to social welfare. Let us strive to make the human race one happy brotherhood of men, in which each life shall be sustained by every other life. Thus Christian Socialists speak, besides a host of others who do not go by that name.

There is more to be said about Christian Socialism. The striking thing about it is that it comes in the name of Christ. It calls itself *Christian*. Jesus, it says, was the world's greatest Socialist. His mission, his only purpose, was to reform society. True Christianity is Socialism. And – don't be shocked! – the second coming of Christ will simply consist of this, that Socialism will reign supreme on earth, that the world will have become one big socialistic state.

Let us consider the question whether Jesus was a Socialist; or, to put it mildly, whether Jesus was a social reformer. That he was, is the fundamental dogma of Christian Socialism. So this matter is all-important.

On the basis of Scripture but one answer is possible. It is a very emphatic *No*. Jesus never raised his voice against corrupt government, though there was abundant occasion in his day. He did tell men to respect the authorities, corrupt though their practices were. 'Render unto Caesar the things which are Caesar's', he said (*Matt.* 22:21). He failed to protest against slavery, though half the people in the Roman empire at the time are said to have been slaves. He never discussed the matter of fair wages for a day's labour. To the contrary, in the parable of the men who came to labour in the vineyard at different hours and yet, at the close of day, all received the same pay, he seems to have laid down a very unjust scale of wages. He never urged the poor to start a savings-account in the bank. Quite to the contrary, he urged everybody to gather a treasure not on earth but in, heaven. The chance of his life to protest against poverty he let slip by. A woman once poured an alabaster box of ointment on him. Judas – mark you: Judas, the traitor! – objected that the money might better have been given to the poor. But Jesus took sides with the woman. True, on two occasions he fed the hungry multitudes with bread and fish. But that gave them only temporary relief, at best for a few hours. And soon after, he rebuked the people for following him because of perishable bread. Again it is true that he spent much of his time healing the sick. But he never launched a campaign for the prevention of any disease. He must have had in mind individuals rather than society. And was it not his custom to dismiss the individuals whom he had healed with the spiritual lesson that they should quit sinning? Bodily succour was Jesus' avenue of approach to the soul.

Is any further refutation of Christian Socialism needed? Did not Jesus declare that his kingdom is not of this world? Did he not, after a brief stay on earth, return to heaven? If he wanted to reform society, he should have remained here. To his followers he said, 'I go to prepare a place for you. And if I go and prepare a place for you, I will come again, and receive you unto myself; that, where I am, there ye may be also' (*John* 14:2,3). And, finally, did he not predict that the present order of society, instead of being reformed by Christianity, would be cast into fire, to make room for a new earth on which righteousness would dwell?

Does it follow that Christians should not at all concern themselves with social problems? Certain Christians, notably the Anabaptists and some Premillenarians incline to think so. But God forbid! It would be easy to show the very opposite from the Word of God. We would gladly prove it if our theme required us to do so. But we may conclude, nay, even must, that the chief interest of Christianity is spiritual, not material; that the first concern of Christianity is not to make men outwardly comfortable now, but to make them perfectly happy eternally. The prime object of Christianity is to prepare sinners for heaven. And the only way to Christianize society is by Christianizing individuals.

Most emphatically, the Christ was not a social reformer. Christian Socialism is not Christianity. It is a deceiver coming in the name of Christ. It is an Antichrist.

Look out for this Antichrist! His power is growing apace. His domain is rapidly being extended. The war has greatly aided his cause. The misery occasioned by the war has caused men to look around for a sure cure. Many, very many, think they have found a' panacea in Socialism. Christian people are turning to so-called Christian Socialism. In the course of the war a great man said, 'Whoever wins the war, Socialism is going to be the big victor.' Whether this prediction is coming true for the political party called by that name may perhaps be questioned. But of the spirit of Socialism it surely holds. So does it hold of Christian Socialism. Religion and the church are being socialized rapidly.

d. Finally we call attention to the very widespread doctrine of the divinity of man.

Who is Christ? we ask. The most pointed answer we can give is: *Christ is God in man.* But is not almost everybody telling us nowadays that God is in every man, that there is at least a spark of divinity in every human soul? What else can this mean but that every man is his own Christ? That follows with absolute necessity. Here then is Antichrist. Here we have the stark naked form of Antichrist.

Would you know when Satan cast the spirit of Antichrist upon earth? When in the garden he told Eve, 'Ye shall be as God.' That spirit has a mighty and almost universal grip on mankind today. For a single illustration, with what satanic boldness it stares at us from the Harvard class poem of 1908, entitled *Man!* We quote only one stanza:

> O holy spirit – O heart of man!
> Will you not listen, turn and bow
> To that clear voice, since time began
> Loud in your ears, and louder now!
> Mankind, the Christ, retried
> Recrowned, recrucified;
> No god for a gift, God gave us,
> Mankind alone must save us.

This manifestation of Antichrist deserves much more than passing notice. It is at once easily his boldest and most seductive manifestation. But rather than enlarge on it now, we choose to warn against it repeatedly in future sermons of this series.

Just one more remark must be made at this time. This greatest of all errors has made considerable headway in the course of the war. So common a thing has it become to place the men who gave their lives for the cause of the allies on a par with Jesus Christ, to parallel their sacrifice with his, that we almost forget to be shocked when we hear this done. Yet how shocking! No matter how noble the cause for which they suffered, the comparison is sacrilege.

Already the apostle John wrote: 'Even now are there many Antichrists, whereby we know that it is the last time.' Nineteen centuries have since rolled by, and Jesus has not yet come. Now too there are many Antichrists in the world, from which we conclude that it is the last time. But is it possible that other nineteen centuries will not yet bring the Saviour's advent? It is not likely. That it is unlikely in the extreme appears from certain striking things about the Antichrists of our day.

Never has the Antichrist had nearly as many followers as today. Consider the four Antichrists of this sermon, and you must admit that almost everybody is following him. Think of just the last Antichrist we spoke of, and you must grant that the world is running after him. 'And shall deceive *many*', says Jesus.

Antichrists have ever *opposed* the Christ. They do so now. But never have they come so boldly *in the name of* Christ as today. With amazingly bold front each of them is saying, 'I am Christ.' What you and I call Christianity, they tell us, is not Christianity at all. *They* claim to be Christianity; nay, the Christ himself. Never in the history of our race has the Antichrist come so openly in the name of Christ.

For that very reason the danger is great that we shall be led astray. Antichrist is doing his utmost to deceive even the elect. If he came and said, 'I am of the devil', we would instantly turn our backs on him. Now that he comes and says, 'I am the Christ', we are inclined to give him an audience.

There is a famous poem entitled *Die Lorelei* by Heinrich Heine. A beautiful woman is seated high upon a cliff at the water's edge. As she combs her golden hair, she sings with wonderful sweetness. By the beauty of her form and of her song mariners are attracted. They can hardly help turning their boat in her direction. But whoever does so is certain to have his vessel dashed against the rocks, and himself to find a watery grave. The present-day Antichrists are Loreleis. Beautiful is their form. Sweet is their song. They come in the name of Christ. But alas for him, yea, seven times alas, who lends his ear to their siren song, his gaze to their female beauty! Destruction is his mother.

It is the last time. *The* Antichrist is ready to appear. When he has come, the last battle between the serpent's seed and the woman's will be fought. The Christ will descend to meet the Antichrist in the arena. Who knows but that some of us may live to witness the struggle? It will be brief. God be thanked, we are assured of the outcome! The Christ will crush his opponent's head. Even now, then, hold ready the royal diadem to crown the Victor Lord of all!

6

Latter-Day
Devil-Worship

Now the Spirit speaketh expressly, that in the latter
times some shall depart from the faith, giving heed
to seducing spirits, and doctrines of devils.

1 TIMOTHY 4:1

*T*HE *SPIRIT* OF OUR TEXT is of course the Holy Spirit of God;
more particularly, the Spirit who guided the holy men of God
in writing the Scriptures; still more particularly, the Spirit of
prophecy.

He is said to have foretold the departure of some from the faith
in the latter times. About the meaning of the last phrase there is a
difference of opinion among expositors. Some say that *the latter'
times* here designate the future in a general way, while others think
the reference is to the times immediately preceding the end. The
matter is easily settled. Even if it be granted that the term, strictly
speaking, designates simply future times, yet we may assume that
the apostle has in mind the period just before the end of time. In
the apostolic age Christians generally expected an early return of
the Saviour. The future and the end were to their minds practically
synonymous.

We arrive at the same conclusion when seeking an answer to
the question what *express* statements of the Spirit the apostle is
referring to. He may have in mind his own guidance by the Spirit

while writing this passage. But surely he is also thinking of earlier predictions. To our mind comes at once the frequent teaching of Scripture that the end will be closely preceded by a great apostasy from the faith. Did not the Saviour sigh, 'When the Son of man cometh, shall he find faith on the earth?' (*Luke* 18:8)? And is not, according to Jesus, the following of many after false teachers a sign of his second coming (*Matt.* 24:5, 11, 24; *John* 5:43)?

Those who depart from the faith will give heed to *seducing spirits and doctrines of devils*. By *seducing spirits*, false prophets are not meant, but the evil, deceiving spirits controlling them. And *doctrines of devils* are not doctrines about devils, but doctrines emanating from, inspired by, devils. Men will give heed to the spirits from the deep, rather than the Spirit from on high. They will follow after the doctrines of devils rather than the doctrines of God.

What doctrines are they that' proceed from devils? We need not hesitate to reply: *all false teachings*. The devil is the father of lies. There never was a lie but it was inspired by him or his associates. Every false teaching is a teaching of devils. Everybody giving heed to such teachings is following after seducing spirits. He who gives up the faith in exchange for such teachings thereby becomes a devil-worshipper.

Time forbids us to attempt to speak on all present-day forms of devil-worship. We shall dwell on a few forms in which the devil is very evident; in which you may easily detect his face, his voice, his claw.

LATTER-DAY DEVIL-WORSHIP is our subject. We call attention to —

    a. Some reasons for the prevalence of devil-worship in the
      latter day.

    b. Some evidence of its prevalence in our day.

a. The worship of the devil will be prevalent just before the end. God tells us so in our text. But the modern man challenges that statement.

Devil-worship was a common thing long, very long, ago. Two thousand years ago, it was taught in India that the spirits of the dead filled the air and could be consulted by the living. The ancient Canaanites were expelled from their land because they practised divinations, enchantments, witchcraft, necromancy, and the like. The Egypt of the oppression had its sorcerers, wizards, and magicians. Just think of Jannes and Jambres, the rivals of Moses and Aaron.

In Babylonia astrology flourished for centuries. The ancient Greeks and Romans worshipped innumerable mysterious spirits. We Christians call all that devil-worship, and that it was. The devil was the prince, nay the god, of ancient paganism. And he will be the god of the future.

Says the modern man: 'I do not believe that a devil exists; there is no such being; and therefore I refuse to speak of devil-worship. But, call it what you will, you surely do not mean to say that man is going to revert to the religion of the ancient heathen! That were an absolute impossibility. That were entirely inconceivable. There has always been evolution in man's religion, and there is today. The religion of each century is far superior to that of the preceding. The religion of the end – if indeed there is going to be an end – will be as far exalted above that of the ancients as your heaven is high above the earth.' Thus the modernist reasons.

Do you not observe that the Christian and what is commonly called the modern view of the religion of the future are squarely opposed to one another? Do you not hear the two clash? The modernist claims that, thanks to evolution, it will be infinitely superior 'to the religion of ancient paganism. The Christian calls both by one name. That name is *devil-worship.*

Of course, the Christian is right. He has the infallible Word of God to bank on. Before we get through, it will appear that actual present-day phenomena also justify him.

We propose to mention some reasons why the worship of the devil must needs be the religion of the end.

We start out from the perfectly safe assumption that this dispensation will end in a period of general unbelief. True believers are going to be few and far between.

In other words, we shall show *that unbelief is bound to end in devil-worship; that he who turns from the Christ, is casting himself into the open arms of the devil; that he who refuses to bow before God will presently be found on both knees before the throne of Satan. It cannot be otherwise.*

The unbeliever rejects the truth. He barters truth for falsehood. Questioning the oracles of God, he lends his ear to God's rival. He does what Adam and Eve did in the garden. They believed the father of lies rather than the God of truth. *Thus they substituted the devil for God.* Thinking that they would themselves become gods, they accepted Satan as their god in reality. The modern unbeliever does the identical thing.

The unbeliever laughs about this reasoning. He laughs until he shakes all over. For all this talk about the devil he regards as old wives' fables. The idea of a personal devil seems so perfectly ridiculous to him that he does not even care to argue against it. He laughs Satan out of court. But by so doing he plays himself into the murderer's hands. The devil can make rings all around the man who scornfully denies his very existence. So he does. He ropes him in. He has him at his mercy.

The unbeliever calls God, who is Truth itself, a liar to his face. Do you think God will brook that? Impossible! He is certain to avenge himself. And how can he do this more appropriately than by assigning the unbeliever to the domain of the real Liar? That he does. God surrenders him unto the power of Satan. We shudder as we make that statement, but make it we must. Twice in his epistles Paul makes mention of his delivering certain individuals unto Satan (*1 Cor.* 5:5; *1 Tim.* 1:20). Most likely he is thinking only of the bodies of these individuals. The delivery of the body unto the power of the devil is already so awful that we marvel as we read about it. But if the unbeliever persists in his unbelief, not merely Paul, but God himself, will deliver him to Satan body and soul. Our hairs rise on end as we think of it. God forbid that it should happen to one of us!

There is still another reason why unbelief is sure to issue in devil-worship. Perhaps it is even more compelling than the reasons already given. It is absolutely compelling. There is no getting away from it.

Man was created a religious being. As long as man is man, he will be a religious being. No tribe has ever been found even in the darkest parts of dark Africa that did not have a religion. An irreligious individual does not exist. An irreligious man were a contradiction in terms. It follows that as soon as man rejects God, the true God, he is going to look around for a substitute. He cannot help it. He must. Now of course he desires a supernatural god. The idea of God and the idea of supernaturalness are inseparable. A god who is not supernatural is no god at all. The unbeliever may deny the existence of everything supernatural, but that makes no difference. His very essence thirsts for the supernatural. And so in his search for a substitute for the true God, he unavoidably turns to God's superhuman rival, the devil. Before he himself is aware of it, he has enthroned the devil in his heart as god. The old saying is true, 'Where unbelief is lord of the house, superstition has already opened the door for itself.' A Reformed theologian has called superstition 'the bastard form of true religion, the caricature of faith' (Herman Bavinck).

Small wonder indeed that fortune-telling, magic, the calling up of the dead, and the like, are met with, surely not exclusively, yet especially, in those circles that boast of their unbelief. To some it may seem surprising that the great infidel Voltaire had a childish fear of unfavourable omens, and on their account often changed his plans. But it would be surprising if this had not been the case. Many people in unbelieving Paris are deathly scared to sit down at the banquet-board in a company of thirteen. It is reported that some Parisians make it their business to be invited out as fourteenth guests.

Unbelief cannot help but end in devil-worship. If God is not your God, the devil is, or he will be very soon. Since the world in the latter days will have rejected God through unbelief, it will be found prostrate before the throne of Satan.

b. As we proceed to call attention to some evidence of devil-worship in our own day, we first of all wish to emphasize the general truth that the devil is a remarkable imitator of God. His policy is one of imitation throughout. From the standpoint of success it is not a bad policy either. Full well the devil knows that God is his superior in every way, also in wisdom. Therefore he adopts the methods which God is wont to employ in drawing men to his service. He reasons that the more closely his religion resembles that of God, with so much the greater ease will he be able to attract men from God's service to his own. To that Paul refers when he warns us to be on our guard against the devil because he transforms himself into an angel of light (*2 Cor.* 11:14).

We come to some outstanding particulars. God has given men his special revelation in the Bible; the devil also gives special revelations to men. One form of divine revelation is that of prophecy, in the sense of the foretelling of future events; Satan's specialization along this line we call soothsaying, fortune-telling, etc. The

God of Israel doeth wonders; Satan is a master in magic. God came to dwell in man; Satan does the same thing. When the incarnate Word was on earth, the Jewish land abounded with persons possessed of demons.

We propose to show successively that *men today in large numbers are turning from the divine revelation to the satanic, from prophecy to soothsaying, from miracles to magic, from the incarnate God to the incarnate devil.*

You have heard of *Theosophy.* Its discoverer was Madame Helena Blavatsky, a Russian lady. After considerable travel through the Orient, she came to New York City, where in 1875 she organized the Theosophical Society. The ideas upon which this society was based were said to have been revealed to her by telepathic messages from certain 'Brothers', dwelling in the inaccessible fastnesses of the Tibetan Himalayas. She posed as their mouth-piece. The 'Brothers', she asserted, far removed as they were from all contact with ordinary men, had, by countless generations of the simplest kind of living and tireless cultivation of their spiritual powers, received an insight into the secrets of nature that no one else could possibly obtain. Their revelations to her she published in a book entitled *Isis Unveiled.* Through this book and through her periodical, *The Theosophist,* she gained thousands of followers. in America, though perhaps her disciples are most numerous in India.

By this time Madame Blavatsky has been exposed as a gross impostress. The letters which were said by her to come from the 'Brothers', and were found sometimes in cushions, sometimes in private drawers, sometimes on trees, while at other times they dropped out of the air, were written by herself. Surely, such deception is the work of the liar from the beginning. Yet there are many Theosophists even at the present day. Our own city of Grand Rapids has the doubtful distinction of harbouring a Theosophical Society.

Joseph Smith, the founder of Mormonism, was born in Vermont in the year 1805. His father was a so-called water-witch. By means of a magic fork he was said to be able to locate hidden streams. Joseph acquired this power from his father. The son advanced beyond the sire. Joseph divined where to find lost articles and stolen goods. At the age of fourteen, Smith began to have visions. In 1820 he saw two angels who bade him have nothing to do with any of the denominations. In 1823 an angel informed him about hidden plates in the hill Cumorah. He was permitted to go and see them. Four years later, the angel Moroni delivered these plates to him. With them was a peculiar stone, Urim and Thummim, by the aid of which they could be translated. The translation constitutes the *Book of Mormon,* the Mormon Bible.

Later on Smith received several other revelations. In 1843 he had the notorious revelation about the so-called celestial marriage. At Independence, Missouri, God revealed to him the location of the New Jerusalem, the place where the temple will be built. When the bank which he managed at Kirtland, Ohio, failed, and the depositors were very much enraged, God was kind enough to reveal it to him that he should depart for Missouri. And Smith was wise enough to obey.

That Mormonism is of the devil is plain as broad daylight. Just listen to a few of its teachings! 'All other churches are wrong; the Mormon church is the only true church on earth', said Smith. The book of Mormon is placed on a level with the Bible. Belief in Joseph Smith is said to be essential to salvation. 'Adam is our God and Father, and the only God with whom we have to do', said Brigham Young, Joseph Smith's successor. God and Jesus are said to have had many wives. Surely, that example ought to be followed. Yet it is conservatively estimated that there are some four hundred thousands of Mormons in the United States at the present time, besides some twenty five thousand elsewhere.

We call special attention to Modern Spiritualism. We say *special* attention because there are reported to be some fifteen millions of Spiritualists in America alone. The number is startling. Think of it: 15 million out of a population of 105 million! One of every seven Americans a Spiritualist! To be sure, the number cannot be definitely verified. It may be an exaggeration. But even at that, the actual growth of Spiritualism in this country, and for that matter the world over, is nothing short of startling. Modern Spiritualism originated with the Fox family at Hydesville, New York, in the year 1848. It teaches the possibility for the living to commune, even to converse, through a medium, with the spirits of the dead. The spirits are said to give information about their condition, the company they are in, and like things. Spiritualists claim that their number has grown rapidly during the war. We believe it. Small wonder that in many cases the relatives of the millions of men who left home not to return, but to be buried on distant fields of battle, should strongly desire to communicate with their spirits.

What are we to think of Spiritualism? How must the spiritualistic phenomena be explained? At least three answers are possible. Taken together they likely cover practically all cases.

It cannot be questioned that there are *powers in nature* as yet undiscovered. There are also powers of the human soul about which we know little or nothing. These hidden powers may produce, undoubtedly often *do* produce, phenomena that strike us as being supernatural, whereas in reality they are quite natural.

That there is any amount of *fraud* in modern Spiritualism is beyond cavil. Fraudulent practices of the Fox sisters have been exposed on more occasions than one. Some students of the subject take the position that Spiritualism is a fake from beginning to end. Now all faking is of the devil.

And then, believers who have made a thorough investigation agree that the spirits with which the media may occasionally commune, are *not spirits of the dead but demons.* One of them has said, 'The Prince of darkness presides at the seance' (G. Wisse). A certain Dr B. P. Randolph, once a medium, says, 'For seven years I held daily intercourse with what purported to be my mother's spirit. I am now fully persuaded that it was nothing but an' evil spirit, an infernal demon.' J. V. Coombs is authority for it that the following prayer was offered in Lyceum Hall, Boston, by Miss Lizzie Doten, a medium: 'O Lucifer, thou Son of the Morning, who fell from thy high estate, and whom mortals are prone to call the embodiment of evil; we lift up our voices unto thee. We know thou canst not harm us unless by the will of the Almighty, of whom thou art a part and portion, and in whose economy thou playest a part, and we cannot presume to sit in judgment over Deity. From the depths of thine infamy streams forth divine truth. Why should we turn from thee? Does not the same inspiration rule us all? Is one in God's sight better than another?'

Did you ever hear of more blatant devil-worship? Anybody who so much as consults a medium takes part in that worship.

Men are turning from prophecy to soothsaying.

The modern civilized world is extremely superstitious. Many dread to launch an enterprise on Friday: it could not succeed. For most people thirteen is an unlucky number; to a few it brings luck. A howling dog under the window of a sick-room means certain death. Hang a horse-shoe over your door! The month in which you were born determines your fortune in life. Athletic teams are dreadfully nervous if they have to enter a contest without their mascot. And any number of people who smile about such things, take much more stock in them than they are willing to admit.

Fortune-tellers abound in the Christian world. It is said that in aristocratic, highly civilized Boston fifteen thousand persons resort to them and pay some half a million dollars annually for the doubtful privilege of prying into the future. Everywhere it is almost impossible to keep these frauds outside the Fairs. Fortune-tellers are the devil's *tools*. Those who consult them are the devil's *fools;* nay, worse than that, his *worshippers*.

And here let us add that he who is not satisfied with the signs of the Saviour's advent as pointed out in Scripture, but attempts to fix the exact date of the great coming event, is in the devil's employ, at least at the time of figuring. That applies to Russell,[1] the Adventists, and a lot of others. Russell, by the way, seems to have worked for the devil about twenty-four hours a day.

Men are exchanging miracles for magic.

There is a heavy demand for sorcery. But rather than enlarge on it, we choose to dwell on the cure by magic of bodily ailments, one of the devil's specialties during the last decades. We have only to mention Christian Science, Emmanuelism, and Dowieism,[2] and you know why we speak of *specializing*.

What must we think of the so-called magic cures effected by one or another of these or like systems?

Some real cures, maybe many, have been brought about by calling into play the influence of the mind on the body. The spirit of man unquestionably has far greater power over his body than most of us surmise. It is a well-known fact that mental depression can make one physically ill. Why should not mental stimulation improve one's physical condition? By emphasizing this truth these systems have rendered mankind a distinct service.

But never swallow the devil's poison just because he would administer it to you in the form of a sugar-coated pill! How much power Satan sometimes may wield, we are not prepared to say. Occasionally, we doubt not, God lends him great power. Whether

---

[1] Charles Taze Russell (1852–1916), founder of a society which later became 'Jehovah's Witnesses'.

[2] Two healing movements of the early twentieth century. The Emmanuel movement relied more on psychotherapeutic techniques, while John Alexander Dowie believed in healing in answer to 'the prayer of faith'.

he is in the habit of using his power to cure the sick, we question. Once in a while he may do this. But it may safely be assumed that, generally speaking, he makes more people sick than well. The story of Job gives us an inkling in that direction. And of this we are absolutely sure: that a very large percentage of supposed magic cures are *fake* cures. And of all fakes Satan is the author.

We come to a matter of utmost importance. When the incarnate Son of God was on earth, Satan imitated the incarnation by sending demons into human bodies. Do not think that he has given up the practice of imitating the incarnation! He still does it. Only, today he goes about it in a way much more subtle and sly.

God in man – that is the meaning of the incarnation. So much is perfectly plain. But now hear what the devil is telling us! God, he says, is in every man. Jesus was incarnate God, to be sure; but so is everybody else God incarnate. Jesus was the Son of God; but so are you the Son of God. That is the present-day satanic corruption of the truth of the incarnation. And it has many more millions of adherents even than Spiritualism. It is believed generally.

Observe the logical conclusion of this greatest of all errors! The Bible tells us that many men are children of the devil. It was the meek and gentle Saviour who called the Jewish leaders by that name (*John* 8:44). Now he who says that all men are God's children, calls Satan's children God's; declares that those whose hearts are filled with the devil, are filled with God. Can you fail to see how Satan is substituting himself for God? The modern man, said to be full of God, but in reality full of the devil, is Satan's imitation of the incarnation.

The imitation is not at all a poor one. But Satan is still busy perfecting it. The error of the divinity of man is going to issue in the Antichrist. He will be the devil's own child. Many think that he will be the devil incarnate in exactly the same sense in which Jesus Christ is God incarnate. We consider this likely. But be that as it may, he surely will deserve the name *Child of Satan* as no one ever deserved it before him. He will be the most nearly perfect imitation of God incarnate that the ingenious devil can devise. And *he* will proclaim himself God.

Those who now preach the error of the divinity of man will, if they still live, be the first to follow after him.

Devil-worship will prevail at the end of time. Devil-worship is becoming exceedingly prevalent in *our* day.

Devil-worship is a sign of the times.

Soon may we expect the Christ to judgment. Then the devil will be cast into the lake of fire and brimstone.

You and I will stand before the great white throne.

Are you ready? Only then are you ready if you *believe*. It is *unbelief* that leads to devil-worship. *Belief* is the very essence of the religion of the living God. So *believe* in the God of the Bible and in his Son Jesus Christ! Then only will you be saved from the devil's worship now, from the devil's company everlastingly.

7

Sleeping Christians

While the bridegroom tarried,
they all slumbered and slept.

MATTHEW 25:5

I N A PREVIOUS SERMON we compared the days of the Son of
man with those of Noah and of Lot. As Noah's contemporaries
and Lot's fellow-citizens were heedless of impending catastrophe, so in the end the world will unexpectedly be overtaken by
destruction. *The Heedless World* was our subject.

Now we wish to take you a step farther. We shall bring the
matter a great deal nearer home. Not only will *the world* be heedless in the latter days, but *the very church of Christ on earth will be
asleep.* That the Saviour tells us in our text. For it cannot be dis-
puted that the ten virgins of the parable represent the church, the
body of professed Christians. *They* nod and fall asleep.

We choose to limit our subject. Of the ten sleeping virgins,
five are wise and five foolish. The wise are true Christians; the
foolish are Christians only in name, not in reality. The wise are
living members of the church; the foolish are *in* but not *of* the
church. Now of the foolish virgins much has already been said in
the sermon on *The Church's Departure from the Faith* (p. 28), based
on Jesus' plaintive words, 'Nevertheless, when the Son of man
cometh, shall he find faith on the earth?' So this time we shall leave
the foolish virgins to one side, and consider only the wise. The

remarkable truth that calls for our attention now is: *that the coming Saviour will find even his faithful followers asleep.*

In this series we are concerned with the *present* rather than with the *future;* with what *is* rather than with what *shall be.* By signs of the times we mean things that may be observed *now.* So you might infer from our choosing Matthew 25:5 as our text that we think that Christ's faithful followers are sleeping, at least slumbering, even now. The inference is quite correct. That is exactly our view.

Do you marvel? Do you say that Christians everywhere are busily talking about the Saviour's second coming? Do you remind us that the market is being flooded with books on his advent? Do you offer to prove the proposition that the church has never yet shown as deep an interest in his return as today? Do you call our attention to it that even many unbelievers are expecting the early arrival of a great deliverer? We see no reason to change our mind.

Observe the context! The virgins are expecting the bridegroom. They have taken their lamps and gone out to meet him. Of course they are talking, busily talking, about the coming marriage-feast. A few moments later they are fast asleep. So you see it is possible to fall asleep while one is out with the express purpose of meeting the bridegroom. Might that not fit the case of many a Christian today?

And then, let us call attention to a striking parallel!

Just before Messiah's first advent, the Jews were anxiously looking forward to his coming. Ah, how they longed for David's son to smash the Roman yoke! The kingdom of God, which they supposed was at hand, was uppermost in their minds, foremost on their lips. It was the talk of the times. Yes, the expectation of the birth of a king of the Jews, who was to be Saviour of the world, had penetrated to heathen lands. In the light of this fact must the coming of the wise men from the East be explained. The Saviour came. But marvellous to say, he was not recognized. 'He came unto his own, but his own received him not' (*John* 1:11). How could that be? This is the explanation: the Jews who seemed wide awake were fast asleep.

The second advent of the Christ is the talk of our times. The war made many a Christian long for that happy event, which will put an end to the world's turmoil, to the suffering of the saints. The expectation of the Deliverer's coming has penetrated even to un-Christian and anti-Christian circles. The Order of the Eastern Star – mark the name! – has adopted this as the very first article of its confession: 'We believe that a great teacher will soon appear in the world, and we desire so to live that we may be worthy of him when he comes.' Does it follow that Christians are wide awake to their Lord's coming? By no means! The opposite may be true. The opposite *is* true. As the Jews were asleep, so are we asleep. History is repeated.

We shall prove our proposition by calling attention to —

a. *Some general phenomena among Christians today.*
b. *Some errors of the Premillenariams.'*
c. *Some of our shortcomings as a Reformed people.*

a. A so-called *spiritual* interpretation of Scripture is making rapid headway. The name is not a good one. It sounds good, but is used to designate something bad. Many passages of the Bible which obviously must be taken at their face value are said not to be literally true, but to have only a spiritual meaning. The story of the Fall of man in the garden is called an allegory. The story of Jonah and the big fish, too, has been completely spiritualized. Jonah, we are told, was of course never in the fish's belly.

This 'spiritual' interpretation is being applied quite generally nowadays to the Bible's predictions of Christ's return. The man Jesus, it is said, will never be seen by the physical eye on the clouds.

But 'the spirit of Christ' is going to gain control over the hearts and lives of men. When that has come to pass, Christ will have come. That will constitute the Saviour's advent.

This error is a grievous one. It is fraught with awful danger for the church. Eventually it is bound to land many a one who is now counted with the wise, among the foolish virgins. Even now the question frequently arises in the minds of the faithful whether, after all, their conception of the Christ's return has not always been a bit too plastic, too realistic. They are finding it hard to keep their eyes open. They are nodding.

Much of the talking, the preaching, and the writing of the last few years about Jesus' return was due to the war. It is well. So momentous an event as the world war should strain our interest in Christ's coming to its highest pitch. Yet a question at once suggests itself. Is it not possible that the war acted merely as a stimulant? May it not be that a reaction is going to set in presently? Is it not easily conceivable that a few years from now Christians will take less interest in the advent than they took before the conflict started? What actually will take place we cannot say. Time will tell. But even now there are certain signs suggesting an answer to the above questions. That answer, we are sorry to say, is affirmative. It looks as if the reaction has already begun. At least a few Christians show symptoms of growing tired of 'all this talk' about Jesus' return.

So much is certain: much of present-day so-called interest in the second advent amounts to little more than curiosity. That such is the case is perhaps best shown by the extensive speculations of ministers of the gospel and others on unfulfilled prophecy, and by the voracious appetite of the public for such speculations. People have been set to wondering who is going to be the Antichrist; several have their candidate picked. Many have taken paper and pencil and tried to estimate in actual figures the approximate date at least of Christ's coming. The difficult book of Daniel and the mysterious book of Revelation are easily the most popular of all Bible books. Ministers galore are preaching on them to audiences that tax the capacity of the largest churches.

Now do not misunderstand! Far be it from us to discourage the proper study of unfulfilled prophecy! But how often it is studied improperly! The interpretation of unfulfilled prophecy requires a large measure of reserve. He who undertakes it has to exercise extreme care in all his statements lest he transgress the bounds of truth. Personal opinions and subjective views are of no value. And to go safely he will usually have to steer clear of particulars and be content with generalities. For this is the rule laid down by God himself – and to it we would call special attention, because it is altogether too often ignored, 'Now I tell you before it come, that, *when it is come to pass,* ye may believe that I am he' (*John* 13:19). *Only in the light of its fulfilment can prophecy be adequately understood.* Recently we heard a minister make the telling remark, 'If prophecy is understood, it is prophecy no more.'

Something else we would emphasize. Much time that is being spent in speculating on unfulfilled prophecy, would be used to better advantage if it were devoted to the study of the actual fulfilment of prophecy in our day. Here the Jews of Jesus' day fell short. They centred their attention on prophecies, the fulfilment of which lay in the distant future. They were blind to the fact that numberless prophecies were being fulfilled right before their eyes. Their very interest in the unfulfilled caused them to overlook fulfilled prophecies. In a word, *they failed to observe the signs of the times.* Jesus rebuked them for that. Many present-day Christians deserve the same rebuke for the same reason.

Christians *talk* considerably about the coming of the Lord. That is admitted. But do they *live* in readiness to receive him? That is quite another matter. Alas, it cannot be said of Christians on the whole! To the contrary, they must plead guilty to the charge of worldly-mindedness. Worldly-mindedness is one of the most outstanding faults of present-day Christians. How seldom do they engage in spiritual conversation! They talk on temporal affairs almost all the time. Meditation on God and godly things is an all-but-lost art. The mad chase after a portion of the world's goods leaves no time for it. How our idea of real pleasure has been corrupted! Though we may not frequent worldly places of amusement, yet we clamour for their substitutes. Mrs and Miss Church-member can hardly be distinguished any longer by their dress from Mrs and Miss Worldling. And to mention just one other bit of evidence in proof of a proposition that really needs no proof, because it is altogether too evident to everybody with eyes to see and ears to hear, is it not becoming ever more customary to measure the prosperity of the church merely in worldly terms of numbers of members, of dollars and cents?

Now if a Christian *talks* about Christ's return but does not *live* with a view to this event, may it not be said that he is talking in his sleep? I would say so.

Finally we call attention to the fact that a large number of Christians are firmly of the opinion that the world is rapidly growing better. They are scattered throughout the denominations, from the most conservative to the most liberal. In the latter they are most numerous. But even Dr James H. Snowden, a Presbyterian Professor of Theology, propagates this view in the concluding chapter of his in many ways excellent book, just out, on *The Coming of the Lord: Will It Be Premillennial?* That we do not agree, needs hardly to be said. This group of sermons may be considered a protest throughout against the view. The difference between those who think the world is growing better and those who hold that on the whole it is becoming worse, is so fundamental that we despair of their getting together. It is our conviction that the eyes of the former have been blinded by the evolutionistic spirit of the age.

b. We all know in a general way what is meant by Premillennialism. Briefly put, it is the doctrine of a thousand years' reign by Christ on earth before the final judgment. It is surprising how generally this view is held by the best Christian people of America. We would hardly be exaggerating if we should assert that American Christianity is Premillenarian. It surely can be said of the leaders of American orthodoxy outside of Reformed circles, and of some within these circles. To mention but a few, such men as Gaebelein, Haldeman, Gray, Rader, and even Erdman of Princeton Seminary, are strong Premillenarians.

We want to say a few good things about our Premillenarian brethren, enough to make it plain that they should surely be classed with the wise virgins.

They mean to be orthodox, thoroughly orthodox. Though many of them err in regard to the very important doctrine of predestination, yet it must be said that in most of the fundamentals of Christian truth their orthodoxy is unimpeachable. Better than that, their orthodoxy is not of the cold, scholastic kind that ours alas often appears to be. It is decidedly warm and spirited. We love to hear a Premillenarian defend the authority of 'the Book'. We admire him as relentlessly he scourges the higher critics. Our heart grows warm as, with all the energy at his disposal, he preaches the glorious doctrine of the Christ's substitutional death. We no longer attempt to restrain our emotions when he proclaims salvation through blood, the precious blood of the Lamb of God.

If we should tell a Premillenarian that he is sleeping while awaiting the Saviour's return, he would look at us with surprise both sad and great. A touch of sadness would dull his fiery eyes, because we, he and I, so well agreed on the fundamentals of Christian faith, would yet have to part company. And startled he would look because he of all men always pressed the doctrine of the second advent into the foreground; because his life surely was controlled by this teaching; because he always felt that of all Christians he was wide awake.

We do not like to tell the Premillenarian that he is sleeping, or even slumbering. We would not say it if we did not have to. But we must, to be true to our trust.

Earlier in the sermon we drew a parallel between the Jews, anxiously awaiting the Saviour's first advent and yet sleeping at his advent, and the Christians of our day, speaking much about the Saviour's second advent but also asleep. That parallel applies especially to the Premillenarians. We are exceedingly sorry to say that there is a striking resemblance between them and the Jews of Jesus' day.

The history of the Premillenarian view tells us that it owes its inception to Judaistic influences in the church. It was introduced by Jewish converts who had found it impossible to divest their minds altogether of Judaisms.

As the Jews confidently expected the Messiah to establish an earthly kingdom, so confidently that the great Teacher found it next to impossible to rid even the twelve of this error: so the great majority of Premillenarians look forward with never a doubt, with the cocksureness of the Jewish scribes, to an earthly kingdom of Messiah.

The Jews thought Jesus and the apostles disrespectful of Jerusalem's temple with the ceremonies performed therein. The trouble was that they failed to see in the Nazarene the fulfilment of the ceremonial law. At least a few of the most consistent Premillenarians actually insist that during the millennium the temple-service at Jerusalem will be restored to its pristine glory.

The Jews have ever drawn a sharp line between themselves and other peoples. A reason, too often overlooked, why they hated Jesus unto death, was that he taught that the kingdom of God would be taken from them and given to nations better than they were. The chief reason why the Jews persecuted the apostles was that they brought the gospel of salvation to Gentile as well as to Jew. The Jews did not want the wall of separation torn down. The Premillenarians, it would seem, are ,building this very wall. They distinguish sharply between Israel and the church. Some would even have us believe that the church, consisting of Gentile converts, is going to spend eternity in heaven, while Israel is to possess the earth as an everlasting inheritance.

The Jews refused to acknowledge Jesus as their King. The Premillenarians do assert that Jesus is King of the Jews, but many of them deny that he is also King over his church. No, we would not class them with the men of the parable of whom the King says, 'These mine enemies, which would not that I should reign over them, bring hither, and slay them before me' (*Luke* 19:27). These enemies erred in heart; the Premillenarians err rather in judgment. But *err* they surely do. Think of it! They deny the Son of God exalted at the Father's right hand, and about to come in glory upon the clouds, as their King!

Finally observe! Because they do not think of Jesus as their King, of themselves as his subjects, they fail to see it as their duty to fight for their King in attempting to bring every sphere of life under his sceptre. Society they do not attempt to save. They despair of saving it. They do not even care to try. God, they say, will save society when Jesus comes. We had better keep hands off. But does it not follow unavoidably that the coming King will find them sleeping on the job?

Ah, how sadly Judaistic is the Premillenarian view of the coming of the Son of man! Our hearts are filled with grief as we consider that beloved brethren in the Lord err so seriously in point of so momentous an event.

c. The measure of our grief is not yet full. It will be added unto. It is not necessary to look to the Premillenarian camp for sleeping Christians. They are numerous right among us, in our own circle of Reformed confessors. It is our sad duty next to call attention to them.

It must not be supposed that the Christians of the first century after Christ were in possession of the carefully thought out system of Reformed doctrine that we possess today. Nothing of the kind is true. Centuries were required to develop the statement of Christian doctrine to such a point that theologians could write the leading confessions. In a word, Christian doctrine has been *developed*. And at once we may add that there is no good reason why it should not be developed further today. Our Reformed confessions: the thirty-seven articles of the *Belgic Confession*, the *Heidelberg Catechism*, and the *Canons of Dordt*, precious heritage though they are, do not necessarily say the last word on Christian truth. They can be improved upon. They can be added to. In fact, this ought to be done.

One part of Christian doctrine in particular ought to be further developed than it was at the time when our Reformed confessions were written. It is the part concerning the events of the latter days. Our standards say very little about them. And now it may safely be concluded from the guidance of divine providence that the duty to develop this part of doctrine has by God been assigned to his people in our age. An important part of our task it is to study eschatology, as theologians call it; the doctrine of events centring about Christ's return.

But now observe a saddening fact! There are Reformed people, and not a few, some of them leaders of Reformed thought, who scorn the special study of this subject. They are perfectly satisfied with the confessions as they are. They seem to regard them almost as perfect as the Bible itself. The confessions, they say, have said all that needs to be said on eschatology. And anybody questioning this, is at once suspected by them of heterodoxy. Now frankly, can those who assume this attitude toward the doctrine of the last things be said to be wide awake?   '

We have sometimes been charged with 'dead orthodoxy'. By that is meant that we are very particular as to having an exact knowledge of the truth, in fact so particular that we spend practically all our time bickering about the precise statement of the truth, and consequently have little or no time left for Christian living, for Christian service. The charge, though usually coming from quarters the orthodoxy of which lies open to suspicion, yet cannot be said to be altogether groundless. How much valuable time have we spent – or shall we say, wasted? – in disputing about Infralapsarianism and Supralapsarianism! How much bitterness that dispute aroused among brethren! A few, who find it difficult to keep up with their times, are still brooding over that issue. We cannot help thinking in this connection of the big question among the Jews of Jesus' day, which was the greatest commandment of the law?

Fellow-Christians of Reformed persuasion, if we were really alert for the coming of the Saviour, we would by no means relegate purity of doctrine to the background, but neither would we lose ourselves in certain small points. Least of all would we permit a difference of opinion on non-essentials to interfere with our esteem of one another. We would become active in works of Christian love, realizing that soon we may stand before the Son of man to be judged according to our *works*.

We call ourselves Calvinists. By the way, if John Calvin could arise from his resting-place, excelling in simplicity, and appear among us, he would sternly command us to look around for another name. We admit that it is exceedingly difficult to avoid using the names Calvinism and Calvinist. They have a history. Yet we are convinced that these names are quite un-Calvinistic. But be that as it may. We hasten on to a matter of great importance.

It is sometimes said that the issue of our day is not Calvinism but Christianity; that the big question is not whether you stand by Calvin, but whether you are a Christian. Such statements are very misleading. They should not be made. The antithesis is a false one. Are not the fundamentals of Calvinism at once the fundamentals of Christianity? Is not Calvinism the highest type of Christianity? In the measure that one is a Christian, in the same measure is one a Calvinist at heart, though perhaps one be not called Calvinist, or wish to be.

Yet those who make the above antithesis have sensed a very deplorable state of affairs among us. While the forces of hell are bending every effort to batter down the very foundations of Christianity, we, small, narrow-minded folk that we are, are debating the question who of us deserve to be called Calvinists and who do not merit the distinction. The recent immigrant from Holland doubts the Calvinism of his Americanizing brother. The minister with a stern disposition questions the Calvinism of his gentler colleague. Those excelling in reasoning power are inclined scornfully to stamp the more emotionally inclined as Methodists. There are two views among us regarding the relation of common and particular grace. Are they essentially different kinds of grace, yet both deserving the name of grace, or are they not? The matter is worth some careful study. But we have by no means reached the point that the holder of either of these views may, with the breath of his mouth, banish the holder of the other from the Calvinistic camp. Yet that is being done.

What ails us anyhow? No wonder people say: I do not care whether I am a Calvinist, so long as I am a Christian. Of course, they should not say it. It is all wrong. But who is at fault? When are we going to realize that it is more than time for us to close our ranks against the mighty, on-rushing forces of Antichrist? When are we going to wake up? *Lord, open our eyes!*

And who can deny the desirability, no, the necessity, of our standing shoulder to shoulder with the people of God in other churches in the fight against Antichrist? The decision of our Christian Reformed Synod of 1918 to join the Federal Council of the Churches of Christ in America indicates that we are beginning to realize this duty. But it cannot be said as yet that we are doing anything like our whole duty in this regard. And that means that our insight into the seriousness of our times is neither as clear nor as deep as it should be.

How few of our Reformed people feel the force of Christ's command always to be ready for his coming! We like to dwell on the things that must still come to pass before the Saviour can appear. Certain things must yet happen. That is true. But do we not see the swiftly moving stream of time? With torrential rapidity it rushes on to empty into the ocean of eternity. Ah, things move as if by electricity!

How much may happen in a single month or week or day, no man can say. But we, slowly moving people, sit sleepily by and do not observe.

A pessimistic sermon; you say. We do not admit it. But if so, then it is a pessimistic sermon on a pessimistic text. The fact is that the text tells us a sad truth: 'While the bridegroom tarried, they all slumbered and slept.'

We hear you say, If all are going to be asleep when Jesus comes, if we know that ahead of time, what is the use of trying to keep awake?

We answer that there are exceptions to every rule. Men, even the people of God, were sleeping when Jesus came the first time.

Yet a few were awake. Just think of aged Simeon and Anna in the temple! We surely may assume that there will be Simeons and Annas when Jesus comes the second time. May you and I be among them!

You say: I do not expect to be an exception. I could not hope to be classed with Simeon and Anna. There is no use in my trying.

But you *must* try. It is God's command. In Gethsemane Jesus' most faithful disciples fell asleep. This gave Satan a chance at them. He took it. Presently we find them in shameful flight. Your adversary, the devil, is walking about now, seeking whom he may devour. So 'be sober, be vigilant' (*1 Pet.* 5:8)! When your eyelids grow heavy, arouse yourself with the words of the prophet: 'Though it tarry, wait for it; because it will surely come; it will not tarry' (*Hab.* 2:3). When you commence to nod, commence to pray! And do you not even now hear the voice of the approaching bridegroom calling, 'Watch'?

8

The Jewish Return to Palestine

After many days thou shalt be visited: in the latter years thou
shalt come into the land that is brought back from the sword,
and is gathered out of many people, against the mountains of
Israel, which have been always waste: but it is brought forth
out of the nations, and they shall dwell safely all of them.

Ezekiel 38:8

That blindness in part is happened to Israel,
until the fulness of the Gentiles be come in.

Romans 11:25

EVER SINCE THE DISPERSION of the ancient people of God,
there has lived in the Jewish heart the hope of a return to the
land of the fathers. The liturgy of the orthodox synagogue
teems with petitions for the return of Israel's ancient glory.

In 1896, Dr Theodor Herzl, a Vienna journalist, published a
book entitled *Der Judenstaat*, that is, *The Jewish State*. For some
time before, a strong anti-Jewish spirit had reigned in continental
Europe. In seeking an explanation of this spirit, Herzl came to
the conclusion that it was caused by the impossibility of the Jews
entering completely into the social life of the peoples among whom
they then lived, without becoming submerged. So he argued that,
in order to preserve their identity, the Jews would have to have a

home of their own. Because he looked at the matter purely from an economic and political, not at all from a religious, point of view, it was immaterial to him where this home was to be. He suggested Argentina or Palestine.

Herzl's book stirred the Jews the world over. As early as the next year, 1897, the first Zionist Congress was held. It drew up the so-called Basel Program, Basel in Switzerland being the place of meeting. This states that it is the object of Zionism 'to establish for the Jewish people a publicly and legally assured home in Palestine'. By choosing definitely for Palestine, the economic-political movement attached itself to the ancient religious hope of a restoration.

Since then, several congresses have been held. Zionism has progressed. When the war began, some hundred thousand Jews lived in Palestine. Now, at the close of the war, it is practically certain that the movement will be crowned with early success. Ezekiel's prophecy concerning 'the land which is brought back from the sword, and is gathered out of many people'; about 'the mountains of Israel, which have been always waste: but it is brought forth out of the nations', is about to come true, is being fulfilled in our day.

Here let it be said that of all Old Testament predictions of Israel's return the one which we chose as our text surely refers to the period shortly preceding the very end of time. Ezekiel makes mention here of 'the latter years which will come after many days'. He is addressing Gog, the chief prince of Meshech and Tubal. His campaign against Palestine is foretold. And it is placed generally by expositors toward the close of history.

THE JEWISH RETURN TO PALESTINE is our subject. We shall consider it:

a. As itself a sign of the times.
b. As the herald of Israel's conversion.

a. Our subject is difficult. It is easily the most difficult of all the subjects we have felt called upon thus far to consider in this series of sermons. Several things render it difficult.

We stand on the boundary line – or at least very near to it – between fulfilled and unfulfilled prophecy. Much reserve must be exercised in any attempt to explain unfulfilled prophecy. Even on crossing the boundary line of fulfilment, considerable caution is advisable.

We have to do with a subject concerning which the Premillenarians speak with much certainty. The restoration of the Jews and their conversion are a Premillenarian hobby. We, not belonging to the Premillenarian school, shall have to exercise care, lest our vision be blurred by prejudice; lest we cast away some truth because it is mingled with much error. It would be a pity to reject gold ore because much more than ninety percent of it is worthless substance.

And then, Reformed theologians are not agreed among themselves on the future of Israel. So, no matter what conclusion we come to, we shall never be able to say that we have all the Reformed expositors, or even all the best of them, on our side. The situation is not pleasant. We shall take special pains to stay on the side of the Word of God.

While the subject is difficult, it was never less difficult of treatment than today. The prophecies concerning the Jewish people are being fulfilled. Of that we are quite certain. In the light of their fulfilment, we are beginning to understand them. It is this fact gives us courage to attack the subject. The same fact makes it our duty to preach on the subject, in treating the signs of the times.

Will the Jews return to Palestine? There you have a question which has been debated by Christians for centuries. Premillenarians have always answered it with an emphatic *Yes*. Many others have replied to it with an almost equally emphatic *No*.

Do you wonder how any earnest student of Scripture can deny the ultimate return of the Jews to the land of their fathers? Do you ask how it can be questioned in the face of Ezekiel 38:8, our text; or of Ezekiel 28:25: 'Thus saith the Lord GOD; When I shall have gathered the house of Israel from the people among whom they are scattered, and shall be sanctified in them in the sight of the heathen, then shall they dwell in their land that I have given to my servant Jacob'; or of a host of other Old Testament passages just as outspoken? Then we reply that it makes a world of difference which method of interpretation is employed: whether the so-called literal or the so-called spiritual. Those who favour the literal interpretation of these prophecies of course come to the conclusion that at some time Israel will return to the land of the fathers. Many, however, prefer a more spiritual interpretation, and hold that the reference of these passages is to spiritual rather than to natural Israel.

The reasons usually assigned for the latter preference seem plausible. If we take these prophecies literally, so it is said, then we must also take literally other prophecies occurring in their context. And that means, for instance, that we shall have to assume that not only Israel will be restored to its land, but that other peoples as well, which in ancient times were its neighbours, such as Moab and Edom, will return to their respective homes. But that seems absurd. Worse than that, we shall be forced to believe that the temple at Jerusalem will be rebuilt and the ancient service of the period of shadows restored. Ezekiel would seem to dwell on this at length in the concluding chapters of his book. But such a restoration would be, to put it mildly, an anachronism for the Old Testament period. So the exponents of the spiritual interpretation of the prophecies speaking of Israel's return to its land argue. And they conclude that, since a literal interpretation of these predictions leads to conclusions which are obviously wrong, therefore the return of the natural descendants of Abraham to Palestine should not be looked for.

Many would have us choose definitely between the literal and the spiritual interpretations so-called of prophecy throughout. But we decline to do so. We have no desire to be caught in this trap. The antithesis is false. No sensible expositor of Scripture follows either to the exclusion of the other. The fact is that literal and spiritual elements lie intermingled in prophecy. A single verse may contain both. Sometimes the two are easily distinguishable. In other cases we shall not be able to distinguish them with certainty until the light of final fulfilment has dawned.

But now we are ready to draw a conclusion. At this late date, the year of our Lord 1919, it cannot reasonably be questioned that the Jewish people will return to Palestine. Their return seems altogether assured. Unquestionably the war, or rather the outcome of the war, will greatly accelerate the movement. The Old Testament predictions of Israel's return to the land of the fathers are coming true literally. They may have a spiritual meaning besides. That is not for us to decide now. At this time we insist upon their actual, *literal* fulfilment.

It has sometimes been objected that Palestine will not be able to contain nearly all the Jews which the world now holds. It has been estimated that there is room in Palestine for' a population of at most two millions. But, according to the *Jewish Yearbook* of 1918, the Jews number about fourteen millions. However, the objection seems rather childish.

The above estimate of a possible population of two millions is based on the assumption that the land contains about ten thousand square miles. But in the days of king Solomon it comprised some sixty thousand square miles, and was therefore six times as large. And then, it is doubtful whether even Solomon reigned from the Euphrates to the river of Egypt, the extent of the land promised to

Abraham (*Gen.* 15:18). If by 'the river of Egypt' the Nile be meant, he did not. Besides, who shall say how thickly the land that once flowed with milk and honey may not be populated after it has undergone up-to-date agricultural improvements?[1] And finally, the strongest advocate of the literal interpretation of the predictions of Israel's return to Palestine does not insist that every last Jew must go. Many Jews remained in Babylon when the seventy years of the exile had expired. Yet the Jews as a people returned. Quite a number may remain in the dispersion when God gathers ancient Israel into the land promised unto Abraham, Isaac, and Jacob, and their seed after them.

Thus the objection is also met that many wealthy and influential Jews from time to time express their unwillingness to move to Palestine. They do not have to go.

We propose next to point out how God has already for some time, but especially of late *providentially* been seeing to the return of the Jews to Palestine.

The fact that the Jews, in spite of centuries of dispersion, have retained their identity, have remained a distinct people, is very remarkable. Everybody admits that. Everybody *has to* admit it. They have often been compared to a stream flowing through mid-ocean without mingling with its briny water. An eminent Christian once was in conversation with an infidel. The infidel demanded proof for the existence of God. The Christian glanced out of the window, saw a Jew passing by, and, pointing to him, said, 'That Jew.' Enough was said. Now surely it is a bit risky to conclude, from the fact that the Jews have ever remained a distinct people, to their return to Palestine. Yet at this late date, when their return seems fully assured, we may confidently affirm that God preserved their identity with a view to their return.

---

[1] In April 2009 the population of Israel was 7.4 million, according to data from the country's Central Bureau of Statistics.

A very striking fact, a sign of the times, it is that not merely the orthodox Jews are interested in Zionism, but the liberal Jews as well. Even those of them who take no interest in Old Testament prophecy are working hard at fulfilling the counsel of God. Herzl, the father of Zionism, as was already remarked, was swayed purely by economic and political considerations, not at all by religious motives.

For some time there was a difference of opinion among the Jews as to where they should settle. They were by no means agreed on Palestine. Herzl suggested Palestine or Argentina. East Africa was also proposed. Once an actual split occurred on the issue of location. A strong faction opposing settlement in Palestine was headed by the famous Israel Zangwill. But behold what has happened! Zangwill secretly returned to the Zionist fold. And by this time the Jews the world over are practically unanimous in the choice of the old promised land as their future home.

By anti-Semitism is meant opposition to, hatred and persecution of, the Jew. For centuries the Jews were driven from city to city, from land to land. They have been packed into rotten ships and sent out to sea, there to drown like rats. Of late years anti-Semitism was especially active in Russia. Most cruelly were the Jews oppressed in that country. And in several other countries anti-Semitism may be said to be smouldering, ready to burst into flames at a slight provocation. The spirit of Haman, the son of Hammedatha, is not yet dead. Now persecution of God's ancient people was, in very large measure, responsible for the birth of the movement known as Zionism. It has been *driving* the Jews Zionward.

During the last decades, there has been evident among the Jewish people a reawakened nationalism. Jews have come to occupy the front ranks in many walks of life. It is said that two-thirds of the names you read upon the signs on Broadway in New York City are Jewish names. Several of the big universities of America

– not to mention those of Europe – are crowded with Jewish students. The first Rhodes scholarship was captured by a Jew. Many of the world's leading musicians are Jews. The Jewish people has produced generals and statesmen. We mention only Napoleon's great marshal Masséna, and Britain's prime minister Benjamin Disraeli. Our own Supreme Court Justice, Louis Brandeis, is a Jew and a leader of the Zionist movement. The Jews are conscious of much latent power. They are beginning to assert it. One direction in which they are asserting it is that of securing for themselves 'a publicly and legally assured home in Palestine'.

It seemed for a while that the world war was going to give a serious setback to Zionism. At the beginning of the conflict, the Zionists had their headquarters in Berlin. Most of the money contributed to the cause had thus far come from European countries. Now much money was deflected from Zionism to the war. It became increasingly difficult to send contributions to Palestine. Thousands of Jews in Palestine, upon refusing to enlist in the Turkish army, were forced to flee the country. .Many were massacred. The Zionist colonies were depopulated. Schools were closed. In a word, it seemed that the war was going to administer the death-blow to the movement.But now observe what really did happen! Observe how God overruled events! *The war was precisely the event which helped the cause of Zionism along more than anything else ever did.* The war brought the realization of the Zionist hope within seeing distance, within actual grasp.

Very soon after the opening of hostilities, a Provisional Zionist Committee was appointed in America. Judge Brandeis became its president. While the Jews of Europe were arrayed over against each other in battle, this committee kept the cause alive, even furthered it. On 2 November 1917, Lord Balfour, British minister of foreign affairs, made the following statement in a letter to Lord Rothschild: 'The Government views with favour the establishment of Palestine as a national home for the Jewish people, and will use its best endeavours to facilitate the achievement of this object.' In the course of the year 1918 the British succeeded in wresting Palestine out of the hands of the unspeakable Turk. .

It is generally admitted that President Wilson's oft-repeated declaration that, after the war, small nations must be perfectly free to develop along national lines, implies an approval of the Zionist movement. He himself has said that it does.

The Zionists were quick to enter their claims at the peace conference. And the fact that Zionism has always been organized on democratic lines, in harmony with the spirit of democracy which is now swaying the world, practically assured, from the outset, the recognition of these claims by the peace-makers.

In still another very real way the war has served to boost the cause of Zionism. For many years before, the Jews had been the world's leading bankers. For a long time too the Jews had been in control of many of the world's leading newspapers. In the course of the war the allies were made to feel more keenly than ever their deep indebtedness to the banks and the newspapers. Without their aid the war could not be won. Through them, humanly speaking, the war was won. Almost might it be said that the Jews won the war. It follows that today they can get pretty nearly anything they ask for.

b. What is the meaning for the kingdom of God of the Jewish return to Palestine? Why should God want the Jews to return to Palestine at this time? That is an important question which we shall now have to try to answer.

Many who used to deny that there would be a return, having been compelled by the actual course of events to revise this opinion, and to admit that after all some such thing might come to pass, now say that the return of the Jews to the land of the fathers will have no particular significance for the kingdom of God, that it will be something purely incidental. This view can hardly be looked upon as the fruit of unbiased thinking. It strikes us as being prejudiced. It looks very much like an attempt to dodge the issue. After all that we have said about the obviously providential guidance of the Zionist movement, it goes without saying that this answer leaves us very far from satisfied.

Is it possible that God intends a national restoration of the natural seed of Abraham for its own sake? Can it be the divine purpose to restore Israel to its former national glory as an end in itself? That answer might be expected from an orthodox Jew, but hardly from a Christian. The Christian view is that Israel after the flesh has had its day. God's purpose for natural Israel was that it should bring forth the Messiah. The Christ was the flower of the Jewish nation. The plant had its end in the flower. Since the Saviour's birth, natural Israel was superseded by spiritual Israel. Believers are the New Testament seed of Abraham.

May it be that God intends the restored Jewish nation in Palestine to become the nucleus of Messiah's empire during his reign of a thousand years on earth, the millennium? That is the view held by very many Premillenarians. But we shall have to reject it also. The same objection applies here that was just raised against the view of the orthodox Jew. An additional objection is that Christ's kingdom is not, and never will be, of this world. The Premillenarian idea – or shall we call it Jewish? – of an earthly kingdom of the Christ is contrary to the spirit of the gospel.

It is commonly thought that Jehovah is going to restore his ancient people to their land in order to manifest his unending faithfulness to the promise which he gave long ago to Abraham, that Palestine would be the *everlasting* possession of his seed (*Gen.* 17:8). We think there is something in that. We cannot see how a student of the Old Testament prophecies bearing on the matter can reject this view altogether. But we have no intention of pressing this point. At best the question is thus answered why God should gather his people together *in Palestine.* To the question why he should gather them *at all* a more complete, a far more significant, answer must be given.

What, pray, may be God's purpose in collecting natural Israel? What is the correct answer to this important query? If only it be remembered that Abraham's seed after the flesh has had its day, the matter becomes obvious. *God is restoring the Jewish people to Palestine in order that presently their national conversion, foretold in the Word, may take place. The Jewish return is God's stepping-stone toward the incorporation of natural Israel into spiritual Israel.*

On that point let us enlarge.

Is there going to be a national conversion of the Jews? We answer most emphatically in the affirmative. True, there was a time when even some Reformed theologians, evidently blinded by prejudice against Premillennialism, denied it. Today, we are happy to say, Reformed leaders are agreed that the Jews – as a nation, of course, not individually – will some day accept Jesus as the Christ.

It is difficult to see how any earnest and capable expositor of Scripture could ever call this truth into question. The Word is so very plain. Of the many passages that might be adduced, we quote but a few. Says God in Zechariah: 'And I will pour upon the house of David, and upon the inhabitants of Jerusalem, the spirit of grace and of supplications: and they shall look upon me whom they have pierced, and they shall mourn for him, as one mourneth for his only son, and shall be in bitterness for him, as one is in bitterness for his firstborn. In that day there shall be a great mourning in Jerusalem, as the mourning of Hadadrimmon in the valley of Megiddon. And the land shall mourn' (*Zech.* 12:10–12). Says Jesus to the Jews: 'I say unto you, Ye shall not see me henceforth, till ye shall say, Blessed is he that cometh in the name of the Lord' (*Matt.* 23:39).

How incontrovertibly plainly Paul speaks on the subject in the eleventh chapter of his epistle to the Romans. The gist of the apostle's argumentation is this: because they rejected the Son of God, a hardening has come upon the Jewish people; but this hardening is neither general nor everlasting: there always will be a remnant according to the election of grace; and after the fulness of the Gentiles shall have been gathered in, the Jews too will be received; for 'the gifts and calling of God are without repentance'. We find the matter summed up in the closing sentence of the twenty-fifth verse, where the apostle says 'that blindness in part is happened unto Israel, *until* the fulness of the Gentiles be come in.' Then follows the much-debated statement, 'And so all Israel shall be saved.' Who are meant by 'all Israel'? Many of those expecting a national conversion of the Jews insist that the reference is to natural Israel. We are not going to urge this point. We do not need to. Whatever the meaning of 'all Israel' may be, a future conversion of the Jewish people is foretold so plainly in Romans eleven as to admit of no doubt.

How natural that, with a view to their national conversion, God should gather the Jews together! It would seem to be a matter of course. If the Jews are to be converted *en masse,* they will have to be found *en masse.*

Surely God could, if he chose to do so, convert the Jews as a people while they live dispersed over the face of the earth. But it is very unreasonable to suppose that he would follow this method. God is wont to work through means. In order to exempt the Israelites from the ten plagues with which he visited Egypt, God caused them to dwell apart in the land of Goshen. He might have exempted them, though they had lived scattered throughout the land. But he chose to work through separation as a means. So God is even now calling forth the Jews from among the nations to impart to them collectively a rich spiritual blessing.

The conversion of the Jews will take but a short time. Jesus has told us that the end will come when – evidently, very soon after – the gospel of the kingdom has been preached in all the world as a witness unto all nations. Romans 11:25 informs us that after the gathering in of the fulness of the Gentiles, in the interim, therefore, between the gathering in of the last Gentiles and the end, the Jews will turn to the Christ. So the Jewish conversion must be a sudden occurrence. Now how extremely unnatural to suppose that all the elect Jews, while scattered about everywhere, will be converted almost simultaneously! Surely, they will have to get together for the occasion!

Before Christ's return, the Christian nations will depart far from the faith; will, in large measure, revert to paganism. That is the plain teaching of Holy Writ. The process is well under way today. Now, again, how extremely unnatural it is to suppose that the Jews, while scattered abroad among paganized Christians, will find the Christ of God! Is not the supposition absurd? How very natural, on the other hand, to assume that, in order to be converted, they will be called forth from the midst of the apostates!

Finally, and conclusively, do not the prophets repeatedly place the conversion of the Jews immediately after their return to Palestine? Zechariah does it in his twelfth chapter. Attend also to these words of Ezekiel: 'For I will take you from among the heathen, and gather you out of all countries, and will bring you into your own land. *Then* will I sprinkle clean water upon you, and ye shall be clean: from all your filthiness and from all your idols will I cleanse you' (*Ezek.* 36:24, 25).

Must we explain that converted Jewry will not stand above the fulness of the Gentiles; that the two will stand on a level; that the Jews, after their conversion, will enjoy no spiritual peerage? That ought to go without saying. In Christ Jesus there is 'neither Jew nor Greek' (*Gal.* 3:28). Some one has pointedly said: 'It is as much opposed to the spirit of the gospel that pre-eminence in Christ's kingdom should be adjudged to any man or set of men on the ground of natural descent, as on the ground of superior stature, physical strength, or wealth' (Charles Hodge).

Hard upon the conversion of the Jews will follow the second advent of the Saviour. That has already been pointed out. According to Matthew 24:14 the end will come when the gospel has been preached to all nations. According to Romans 11:25 Israel's blindness will be lifted after the fulness of the Gentiles has come in.

The time of Israel's redemption has not yet come. It cannot be said that the Jews are now turning to Christ. But it is becoming increasingly evident that the stage is being set for this event. The gospel is very rapidly completing its course around the globe. Zionism is meeting with a success that surprises its most ardent advocates. Add the fact that for some time already the Jewish prejudice against Christianity has been showing signs of breaking down. And then attempt to answer the question, whether the fact that they are to receive the land of their fathers back at the hands of Christian nations may not serve to draw the Jews toward Christianity. Surely, even aside from the last two considerations, the exact weight of which it is admittedly difficult to determine, we may conclude, we *must* conclude, that the conversion of the Jews can be looked for before long.

Why has God reserved the conversion of Israel for the very last days? Paul answers that question in Romans eleven. The hardening of Israel is its penalty for the killing of the Prince of life. Because that sin was so very heinous, the penalty is severe. *Long, very long*, will Israel's hardening continue. It will last *clear to the last days*. Of all the nations of the earth, Israel will be the last to find the Christ.

Yet Israel's sin was not unpardonable. 'And now, brethren, I wot that through ignorance ye did it, as did also your rulers', said Peter

(*Acts* 3:17). Did not the Saviour himself, while hanging on the tree, make intercession for the transgressors in the words, 'Father, forgive them; for they know not what they do' (*Luke* 23:34)? The Father, who always hears the Son, will grant this petition in the last days.

And then will appear, as never before, the riches of divine grace, the saving power of the blood that flowed on Calvary. The very people that called out, 'His blood be on us and on our children', will find salvation in that blood. *Wonderful!* WONDERFUL! *Then do you not think that YOU might find salvation in that blood?*

9

The Consolidation of Humanity under Antichrist

And I stood upon the sand of the sea, and saw a beast rise up out of the sea, having seven heads and ten horns, and upon his horns ten crowns, and upon his heads the name of blasphemy. ² And the beast which I saw was like unto a leopard, and his feet were as the feet of a bear, and his mouth as the mouth of a lion: and the dragon gave him his power, and his seat, and great authority. ³ And I saw one of his heads as it were wounded to death; and his deadly wound was healed: and all the world wondered after the beast. ⁴ And they worshipped the dragon which gave power unto the beast: and they worshipped the beast, saying, Who is like unto the beast? who is able to make war with him? ⁵ And there was given unto him a mouth speaking great things and blasphemies; and power was given unto him to continue forty and two months. ⁶ And he opened his mouth in blasphemy against God, to blaspheme his name, and his tabernacle, and them that dwell in heaven.
⁷ And it was given unto him to make war with the saints, and to overcome them: and power was given him over all kindreds, and tongues, and nations. ⁸ And all that dwell upon the earth shall worship him, whose names are not written in the book of life of the Lamb slain from the foundation of the world.
⁹ If any man have an ear, let him hear. ¹⁰ He that leadeth into captivity shall go into captivity: he that killeth with the sword must be killed with the sword. Here is the patience and the faith of the saints. ¹¹ And I beheld another beast coming up out of the earth; and he had two horns like a lamb, and he spake like a dragon. ¹² And he exerciseth all the power of the

first beast before him, and causeth the earth and them which dwell therein to worship the first beast, whose deadly wound was healed. [13] And he doeth great wonders, so that he maketh fire come down from heaven on the earth in the sight of men, [14] and deceiveth them that dwell on the earth by the means of those miracles which he had power to do in the sight of the beast; saying to them that dwell on the earth, that they should make an image to the beast, which had the wound by a sword, and did live. [15] And he had power to give life unto the image of the beast, that the image of the beast should both speak and cause that as many as would not worship the image of the beast should be killed. [16] And he causeth all, both small and great, rich and poor, free and bond, to receive a mark in their right hand, or in their foreheads: [17] and that no man might buy or 'sell, save he that had the mark, or the name of the beast, or the number of his name. [18] Here is wisdom. Let him that hath understanding count the number of the beast: for it is the number of a man; and his number is Six hundred threescore and six.

REVELATION 13

*I*T GOES WITHOUT SAYING that we shall not be able in a single sermon to make a detailed study of so important and difficult a chapter as the thirteenth of the Book of Revelation. We have no such intention. We wish to centre your attention on the one big general truth taught in this portion of Scripture.

At the end of time humanity will be consolidated. Humanity – the elect alone excepted – will unitedly follow after the beast. Says John, '*All the world* wondered after the beast' (3); 'power was given him over *all kindreds, and tongues, and nations*' (7); '*all that dwell upon the earth* shall worship him, whose names are not written in the book of life of the Lamb slain from the foundation of the world' (8); 'and he causeth *all, both small and great, rich and poor, free and bond,* to receive a mark in their right hand, or in their foreheads' (16).

What manner of power, we ask, will succeed in holding the human race together? The beast will do it, aided by his prophet. Now the beast is Antichrist, who, as Paul informs us in the well-known second chapter of his second Thessalonian epistle, will as God sit in the temple of God, showing himself that he is God. In a word, he is the personification of the idea that man is God. *The doctrine of the divinity of humanity will in the end prove to be the mighty consolidating power among men.*

Adam's sin broke the unity of our race. Ever since, man has been attempting to restore unity. But God has his mind made up that man is going to fail. The unification of humanity is work for God, not for man. God is going to effect it through his Son. So the history of the world consists of the attempts of men to consolidate their race, and of God's repeated overruling of these attempts.

This history contains two epochs.

The first ended with Christ's first advent. It seemed that man had succeeded. From the 'eternal' city on the yellow Tiber, proud Caesar Augustus held sway over the whole of the then-known world. But then it was that God set a-rolling the stone which was to crush the kingdoms of earth, and itself to grow until it should fill the earth.

The second epoch will end with Christ's second advent. Again it will seem that man has succeeded. Antichrist will seem to have brought about the unity of humanity. This time not merely the *spirit* of Antichrist, which has been working throughout history, will be manifest; but the *personal Antichrist* will put in his appearance. His victory will seem complete. He will celebrate his triumph. But then the Christ will suddenly appear upon the clouds. The kingdom of Antichrist, seemingly a perfect globe, he will dash into a thousand pieces. And the elect, both living and dead, who constitute the core of humanity, the real human race, he will gather from the four winds into his own perfect kingdom.

We purpose in this sermon to show that the spirit of Antichrist is rapidly completing its work, so that in the near future we may expect the appearance of the Antichrist himself, in whose immediate wake the Christ is coming.

We have to do with what may be called *the* sign of the times. It is more, much more, than a sign among the signs. It is easily the most remarkable of our day. No matter where you look, you see it, if you have eyes to see. It is evident in practically all the important movements of the times. As Philip Mauro says in his much-read *The Number of Man:* 'All our studies of the important movements of the present day will tend to confirm the conclusion that their most striking and permanent characteristic is the pursuit of the ideal of the Consolidation or Federation of all human affairs and interests; that is to say, the formation of a single organization or body; and that the ideal of all these movements is the same, whether the proposed Unification be called *Humanity, Society, Man, Democracy,* the *Brotherhood of Man,* or by some other name.'

We can in this sermon study only a limited number of these movements. The choice is simple. We of course select those which are prominent in Revelation thirteen. And, mayhap to your surprise, you will observe that precisely the movements which stand out in this chapter of Scripture have received a powerful forward-push in the world war just completed. So we are going to study the Consolidation of Humanity *as pictured in Revelation thirteen* and *as furthered by the war.* These are two ways of saying the same thing.

The movements we refer to are three in number: economic, political, religious. Our theme is: THE CONSOLIDATION OF HUMANITY UNDER ANTICHRIST.

Our divisions are —

a. Economic Consolidation.

b. Political Consolidation.

c. Religious Consolidation.

a. 'And he causeth all, both small and great, rich and poor, free and bond, to receive a mark in their right hand or in their foreheads; and that no man might buy or sell, save he that had the mark, or the name of the beast, or the number of his name.' So we read in our chapter, verses 16 and 17.

This passage has sometimes been applied to our present-day labour and trade unions. The mark of the beast has been said to refer to the union button, badge, or label. Though we are not prepared to take the extreme position that no Christian may be member of a union in which unbelievers preponderate numerically, yet we admit that there may be a correct element in this interpretation. We do not set it aside as altogether erroneous. So much is certain: the unions are playing an important part in the consolidation of humanity. It seems that they are going to play an even greater part in the future. Their influence is waxing. The American Federation of Labor has already begun practically to dictate legislation. Yet the application of the passage just quoted must be much wider. It points to an economic consolidation at the end of time on a much larger scale.

An important outcome of the war is the removal of economic barriers. Though the peace conference has not seen fit to go as far in this matter as it seems was the desire of President Wilson, yet it has gone a considerable distance. Many economic barriers are being broken down. The outcome will be that at least some of the commercial rivalry among the nations, which has characterized the past, will be done away with. Commerce, in a sense, will be internationalized. The world over, it will be subject to practically the same rules and regulations. We shall speak less of the commerce of Japan, the commerce of Great Britain, the commerce of America; much more of *world* commerce.

Why was our President so intent upon the removal of economic barriers that he made this one of his famous fourteen terms of peace? It was one point, and an important one, in his programme designed to render war impossible. The President realizes, as every thinking man must realize, that the past war was a commercial one, that its deep underlying cause was commercial rivalry between the leading European states. Now get rid of this rivalry, and the danger of future wars will be greatly lessened. That is sound reasoning. It cannot be denied. We are wholeheartedly with the President. And yet, has it never occurred to you that, when he speaks of continued world peace, his conception of man is a bit too idealistic? To us it seems that he sometimes loses sight of the fact of man's total depravity. The question occasionally bobs up in our mind whether he has succeeded in evading altogether the spell of the modern doctrine of man's divinity.

A prime essential for the unity of our race is oneness of language. The story of Babel's tower teaches that. To break up their unity, God confused the speech of men. Alexander the Great had a deep insight into this matter. Therefore he made Greek the language of his world empire. The Romish church realizes the unifying power of a single language. Latin is used officially in the church the world over. Of late the American government has been waking up to the same truth. It is beginning to look askance at the use of foreign languages in our country. It is right. Not after the notorious manner of Governor Harding of Iowa, but wisely, yet firmly, the government ought to urge upon all American residents the necessity of their learning the language of the land.

Oneness of language is a prime essential particularly for consolidation of the world's trade. If men are going to have business dealings with one another, they must be able to converse. The war has answered the question which language is going to be the language of commerce. It will not be German. Neither will it be that artificial language of which so much was heard a few years ago: Esperanto. Just because of .its artificiality it cannot possibly take. It is not a living language and never can be. But it will be the English language.

In the field of economics two mighty forces are marshalled over against each other. You already surmise what we have in mind. Of course the reference is to Capitalism and Socialism.

It is a notable fact that the war has strengthened *both* of these forces. Many capitalists made tremendous war profits. The number of millionaires was multiplied. Several millionaires grew into multi-millionaires. And if you would witness the growing power of Socialism, just observe how Bolshevism, which is an extreme form of Socialism, is controlling part of the world, and making its influence felt over the whole world. The air is saturated with the spirit of Bolshevism. Sometimes it looks as if Bolshevism might soon engulf the earth.

Everybody knows that Capitalism and Socialism are fighting each other bitterly. It might therefore seem that the world is still very far from economic unity. More than that, one might be led to think that economic consolidation is a mere phantom, never to be materialized. Some one says: 'The reconciliation of Capitalism and Socialism is unlikely in the extreme; neither does it seem possible that either will ever succeed in totally vanquishing the other; and so I think that the economic split of the present will continue to the end.' But our text tells us that it will not. And after all it is not so very difficult to see how present economic strife may issue at an early date in unity.

On the one hand it is quite possible that Capitalism and Socialism, both strengthened by the war, will now prepare for a decisive conflict in which one or the other will go down to complete defeat. Many students of Scripture think that this is going to happen, and they hold that James has foretold in his epistle the downfall of Capitalism in the struggle (*James* 5). We are not so sure of this latter point. But of this we are certain: *whichever side comes out the victor, the spirit of Antichrist will triumph.* For the spirit of Antichrist is manifest in both alike.

Capitalism is rapidly advancing toward a complete monopoly of all business. Big business is crowding little business to the wall. The inevitable outcome will be one big business. As early as 1889 one of our magazines stated: 'It is the big fish eating the little fish, the survival of the fittest. And the logical end must be that every industry in the country will finally be owned and controlled by one huge trust.' In the year 1919 we hasten to substitute the phrase *in the world* for 'in the country'. Now would not the head of that world trust make a pretty good Antichrist?

That the spirit of Antichrist controls Socialism is as evident. Just listen to a few articles of a socialist creed! 'Socialism is the evolution of the human race from the infamy of the swine to the splendour of God.' 'Socialism is the Kingdom of Righteousness.' 'Socialism is the Trinity of Love, Justice, and Truth.' 'Socialism is the Gospel of the Atonement of Humanity for man's inhumanity to man.' 'Socialism is the second coming of the *Elder Brother.*' Comment is superfluous. Never did the spirit of Antichrist speak more boldly!

Do you not see then that, no matter who comes out the victor, whether Capitalism or Socialism, in either case the prophecy of Revelation thirteen' regarding economic unity under Antichrist will be fulfilled?

But just because the *same* spirit is manifest in both of these forces we question whether they ever will come to a final clash. Much rather do we look for it that one is going to help the other along. Do you consider that unlikely? Do you think it impossible? But it is suggested by happenings right before our eyes. Did not capital build up all kinds of big industries before the war? Did not many capitalists deem the war necessary for the protection of their interests, and therefore urge their governments on to it? Did not governments in the course of the war assume control of many of these industries. And is there not a powerful movement on foot now for the continued government control, even ownership, of some of them? This at least suggests how Capitalism may unwittingly play into the hands of Socialism. For what does government ownership of heretofore private industries mean if not a big step in the direction of Socialism? And are there not indications that, if not Capitalism and Socialism, at least capital and labour are getting together? It is becoming quite the thing for employers to give their employees a fairly equitable share of their profits.

b. That Revelation thirteen speaks of the *political* consolidation of humanity under Antichrist is generally granted. We are told about it in plain language. The beast has 'seven *heads* and ten *horns,* and upon his horns ten *crowns*' (verse 1). The dragon gives the beast '*his power and his seat and great authority*' (verse 2). His followers say, 'Who is like unto the beast? Who is able to make *war* with him?' (verse 4).

Quite a number of people, having read what our chapter says about the political consolidation of the human race under a great head, predicted that Germany would win the war, and not only this war, but also several others to be fought in the near future, so that ere long Germany would have subdued the whole world and the German emperor would sway his sceptre over all men. Some went so far as to venture the opinion that Kaiser Wilhelm II would be the Antichrist, the beast of our text.

Now observe what actually did happen! Germany and the Kaiser went down to ignominious defeat. America and the allies won the most complete victory ever gained in the history of human warfare. And that means that for a long time to come we shall have no world empire. In fact there are many more independent nations on earth today than before the war. Erstwhile mighty empires have been split up. The world seems farther removed from political consolidation than ever. The fulfilment of Revelation thirteen seems postponed indefinitely.

Don't you believe it! It may seem so, but it is not really so. Looks are deceiving. The fulfilment of Revelation thirteen is approaching rapidly.

Do not suppose that the world will ever be consolidated politically by *conquest!* No such thing will happen. No such thing *can* occur. Everybody ought to know that by this time. If the Kaiser did not know it, he lacked common sense. Were the world conquerors Nebuchadnezzar, Cyrus, Alexander, and Julius Caesar able to hold their dominions together? Of course not! Their empires crumbled almost as soon as they formed them. Why? Because many of their subjects were unwilling subjects. Perhaps the majority of them were looking for a chance to revolt. And that is bound to be the case in every empire established by conquest. So we dare say that political consolidation resulting from conquest is no consolidation at all.

The spirit of Antichrist has learned that lesson. Therefore he pursues an entirely different policy now from that of ancient times. Now he is going to form a real consolidation. He plans to draw the nations together not by force but by *persuasion. Willingly* they are going to get together. In the end all the world will wonder after the Antichrist, *worshipping* him, as our text says. In a word, it is going to be an *idea*, A GENERALLY ACCEPTED IDEA, that will bring the nations into political union.

Do you wonder what that idea will be? Revelation thirteen gives an answer. The war gives an answer. And these two answers are one.

Our text tells us that it will be the antichristian idea, the idea that man is God, the idea of the divinity of humanity. For the beast is simply the personification of that idea. It will hold sway over all kindreds and tongues and nations (*Rev.* 13:7).

The war tells us that the idea of democracy is to weld the nations together. Did not the war end in the complete triumph of democracy? Is not a league of nations being formed on the basis of democracy? The big democracies have a controlling interest in it, and only self-governing peoples can join. Is it not wonderful that that nation which has so long kept itself aloof from world politics, earth's greatest republic, America, has now stepped forth as the champion of democracy, the chief exponent of the idea of a league of democracies? Surely, not by power, nor by might, but by the spirit of democracy will the nations be consolidated.

We said that the answer of Revelation thirteen and the war's reply to the question which idea will weld the nations together, are one. Does it follow that the spirit of democracy is the spirit of Antichrist? To that important question we answer *No* and *Yes*.

There is considerable confusion as to the real meaning of *democracy*. Some mean one thing by it; others quite another. There is a biblical democracy and an unbiblical. There is a Christian democracy and an antichristian. Let us briefly compare the two.

The basic principle of Christian democracy is *the sovereignty of God.* From it several principles are derived, among them the following. Since God created individuals, instituted families, and organized society before he established governments; therefore there are personal, family, and social rights with which no government may interfere. All men are equal in the sense that no man may of himself assume lordship over his fellows. Might, for instance, is not right; neither is wealth. Only then may one man rule over another when the sovereign God is pleased to lend him authority. Again, government without the consent of the governed is tyranny. In lending authority to certain individuals, God does not ignore the people over whom they are to exercise authority. God vests authority in rulers through the instrumentality of their subjects.

That is why Saul and David, even after having been anointed at God's command, had to be chosen by the people.

The basic principle of antichristian democracy is the sovereignty of the people; that is, the doctrine that the *ultimate* source of authority is in the people, not in anything or anybody else, not in God either. Now do you not plainly see the spirit of Antichrist in this view of democracy? The Christian says: *God is sovereign.* The holder of this view says: *The People are sovereign.* He obviously substitutes man for God. He calls man God.

Now which kind of democracy is holding sway in the world today? Oh, that we might answer unhesitatingly, Christian democracy! But can we? Which do we hear spoken of more often: the sovereignty of God, or the sovereignty of the people? How many newspaper editors, magazine writers, authors, derive popular rights from God? How *few!* Who, when discussing the matter of authority in government still mentions the sovereign God? Only an occasional crier in the wilderness. Yes, the early colonists – many of them – were irreproachably sound in their view of democracy. And well may we thank God for it that several Colonial ideas of government are still lingering in America. But alas! the fundamental religious idea is fast disappearing. Rapidly is it being effaced by the flood of humanistic ideas rushing into our land from Europe, ideas once embodied in the notorious French Revolution. And they are thoroughly antichristian.

And by the way, is there not more than a suggestion in the fact that women's suffrage, which – we are unable to see it any other way – is subversive of divine ordinances, is an outgrowth of the present-day conception of democracy? May not the tree be known by this fruit?

c. Revelation thirteen predicts the *religious* consolidation of humanity under Antichrist. Antichrist himself will be the *God* of our race. 'All that dwell upon the earth will *worship* him' (*Rev.* 13:8). The beast coming up out of the earth (verse 11) is elsewhere called 'the false *prophet*' (*Rev.* 19:20). Now a prophet is surely a religious functionary. This particular prophet is the chief assistant of Antichrist. By means of the *miracles* which he performs he persuades men to *worship* the *image* of the beast (*Rev.* 13:13–14).

Even before the war it was very evident that the world was drifting toward one religion, the religion of the Antichrist. Today, the war having given the movement a mighty push, the blind may almost see.

The days of Protestant denominationalism seem numbered. Have you read the views of the leading ministers of the land on 'the church after the war', as expressed in several issues of *The Christian Herald*? We mention only this periodical because it is widely read. But the whole religious press is groaning under dissertations on the subject. Religious leaders in America are agreed that one of the most prominent results of the war is going to be the wiping out of many denominational boundary lines. They are right. The great majority of them hold that the sinking of denominational differences is desirable. Now *we* are not ready to allow our denomination to be swallowed up. We claim to stand for something distinct and distinctive. We maintain that we have a reason for separate existence, and a good one. Yet is it not generally known that the differences among many of the denominations are so superficial that they could be sunk in quarter of an inch of water? There is no good reason why these churches should not get together. They are going to.   /

There is every reason to believe that the partition separating Protestantism and Romanism will soon disappear. It is full of breaches now. For several years the call 'Back to Rome!' has been resounding in the Protestant churches. Many members of the Church of England have already been received back into the bosom of Romanism. And then there is a strong party in the Romish church which is perfectly agreed with the so-called progressives, the liberals, among Protestants. We refer to the 'Modernists'. Says Newman Smyth: 'They are influenced by one of the profoundest and most vitalizing faiths which are now pervading and renewing the Protestant world. In its simplicity this is the belief that *God is in man.*' Again he says: 'In this faith in God's manifestation of himself in and through human experience progressive Catholics are certainly in the same stream that has vivified and renewed our modern theology.'

We dare go a big step farther. The time is drawing nigh that not merely the Protestant denominations will be consolidated; that not only Protestantism and Romanism will get together; but that *the religions of the world will be united.* Paganism, Mohammedanism, Judaism, and Christianity will be melted into one.

As early as 1892, at the World's Fair in Chicago, a congress of religions was held, which put the Christian religion in a class – perhaps at the head of the class, yet in the same class – with other religions. Has not our own country, our Christian America, for years already had a Buddhist temple in its biggest city? Is it altogether insignificant that in the war Christian nations were allied with Mohammedan and Pagan? Is there not an inkling at least of future events in the fact that in the United War Work Campaign at the close of 1918 we were asked to contribute to the Jewish work as well as to that of the Young Men's and Young Women's *Christian* Associations? Far more significant is the fact that professors of Comparative Religion at our big Universities generally scorn the distinction between the true religion and false religions. The prediction is coming true that the religious movements of the world will 'more and more come to see that their lines of development run parallel, and be therefore induced to federate themselves into even greater union, until at last the time must come when a single world-federation of religions, *the Church of Man*, will rise out of the ruins of the ancient faiths' (Rodolphe Broda).

Earnest Christians have long looked upon the secret orders as rivals of the church. They *are* rivals of the true church. We hesitate not to call them the devil's imitation of God's church, Antichrist's imitation of the Christian church. But nowadays the church and the orders are getting together. We are growing accustomed to hearing the two mentioned in one breath as organizations of a kind. The lodges are quite church-like; and the churches are rapidly becoming more lodge-like. Many leaders in the church hold high degrees in the orders. Is it not possible, even likely, that the secret orders will find a place in the church of the future? We merely ask the question. It at least offers food for thought.

What will the religion of the future be like? Even a casual observer of the signs of the times can answer that question. It will be *the Religion of Humanity*. That is the teaching of Revelation thirteen. It also follows from what has just been said about the actual getting-together of churches and religions in our day. 'Most of the churches are tending toward the religion of humanity,' is a recent statement by Commissioner of Education Claxton.

The divinity of man will be the most fundamental dogma of this religion. That dogma lies at the bottom of most of the talk you hear about the Universal Fatherhood of God and the Universal Brother-hood of Man. On the basis of the same dogma it is asserted that the men who nobly gave their lives in the war on the side of righteous-ness were saved. They are said to have died for humanity. So they did. We honour them for it. Only humanity is not God. When it comes to the point, they made the same sacrifice that Christ made on Calvary; so we are told. 'They completed the suffering of Christ', a minister of the gospel recently asserted.

The Religion of Humanity will be the religion of the future; as things look today, of the near future. The logical. head of that religion will be the Antichrist, who, though man, will sit in the temple of God, showing himself that he is God.

Does it seem unbelievable that one man will stand at the head of so colossal an economic, political, and religious combination, a combination embracing the whole world? Then remember that *it is God who will bring this to pass.* God will give the beast power. Revelation thirteen tells us that repeatedly. Four times we read the expression *it was given him.*

But why will God do that? We give a threefold answer.

God will do it to punish the world for its wickedness. Because it refused to recognize Christ as King, God will surrender the world unto the power of Antichrist.

God will do it to purge the church. And be assured that it will be purged! When the whole world wonders after the beast, it will require the faith of a Daniel, of a Shadrach, a Meshach, and an Abednego, to say *No.* Those who refuse to follow the beast will be persecuted and killed (*Rev.* 13:7,15). Do you doubt that the dross will be separated from the gold? So thoroughgoing will the purging process be that only the elect of God will continue faithful, those whose names are written in 'the book of life of the Lamb slain from the foundation of the world' (verse 8). Are you ready for the fiery trial? It is time you were. The command is about to go forth to fire up until the furnace burn seven times hotter than ever.

God will do it to magnify his Christ. When the Antichrist shall stand at the very pinnacle of power, when he shall be exalted unto heaven, then all of a sudden the Christ will descend from heaven and cast him down to hell. His followers will follow him. The elect will be received in glory. Great voices will say: 'The kingdoms of this world are become the kingdoms of our Lord and of his Christ; and he shall reign for ever and ever' (*Rev.* 11:15).

10

Christian Optimism

And when these things begin to come to pass,
then look up, and lift up your heads; for your
redemption draweth nigh.

LUKE 21:28

WE DESIRE TO PREACH a sermon that may serve as a fitting conclusion for this series on *the signs of the times*.

You surely know by this time that the view which we take of conditions in general on earth at present, does not excel in brightness. Maybe you are ready to jump at the conclusion that our interpretation of the times is quite pessimistic. Of this we are certain: almost any unbeliever would call us thoroughgoing pessimists. Worldly people like to think of Christians as rather long-faced anyhow.

It is this charge of pessimism that we wish to refute.

Do not think for a moment, however, that this sermon is going to be couched in apologetic language; that it will be characterized by an apologetic tone. Nothing of the kind will be the case. We hope to rise far above that. We are not going to show merely that the Christian view of the state of affairs in the world is not pessimistic. Much less shall we rest satisfied after proving that, though perhaps a bit pessimistic, we Christians are not nearly as much so as some imagine. Least of all do we intend finally to brighten up here and there the – on the whole – dark picture which we painted.

We shall leave it exactly as it is. But we propose to show that *the Christian, while taking this exceedingly far from bright view of things, is at the same time the world's biggest optimist.*

CHRISTIAN OPTIMISM is our theme. Our text calls attention to:
a. Its sure foundation.
b. Its grand manifestation.
c. Its early justification.

a. We may differentiate between the objective and the subjective foundation of Christian optimism. The objective foundation is constituted by the promises of God as contained in his Word; while the subjective consists of the Christian's faith in these promises. For our present purpose, however, there is no great need of trying to keep the two apart in our minds.

The Christian believes the providence of God. He sees the hand of God in every event: small or great, good or evil. Nothing ever gets away from God. It is difficult to surpass the definition of divine providence given in the *Heidelberg Catechism*. It is said to be 'the almighty and everywhere present power of God, whereby, as it were by his hand, he upholds and governs heaven, earth, and all creatures; so that herbs and grass, rain and drought, fruitful and barren years, meat and drink, health and sickness, riches and poverty, yea, and all things, come not by chance, but by his fatherly hand' (*Question* 27). Still more beautiful, positively stirring, is the practical conclusion drawn: 'That we may be patient in adversity; thankful in prosperity; and that in all things which may hereafter befall us, we place our firm trust in our faithful God and Father, that nothing shall separate us from his love; since all creatures are so in his hand, that without his will they cannot so much as move' (*Question* 28). Is it not a foregone conclusion that he who says that and means it, must be a full-fledged optimist? We fail to see how he could help being one.

It is the Christian's belief that everything that comes to pass, God causes to come to pass *with a view to the end*. The providence of God ever has been, is now, and always will be, aiming at the end. When the Creator, amidst the singing of the morning stars together, and the shouting of his sons for joy, caused the earth to sink down upon its foundations, then already he had in mind the end. Never is the end out of the divine mind. Only when constantly remembering that can we begin to understand why the Ruler of the universe allows so many things to come to pass that are directly contrary to his revealed will and seem extremely detrimental to the best interests of his kingdom. In the end it will appear that everything helped to hasten the end. And the end will mean the honour and the glory of the Highest. In that light the Christian regards all events, including current events. Do you wonder that his optimism cannot be shaken?

In our text the Saviour asks us to look at the end from a particular point of view. He desires that we think of it as *the time of our redemption*.

Possibly the question occurs to some whether it is not a bit selfish to regard the end from that viewpoint. Of course, in deference to the Word of God, we repress the question immediately upon becoming aware of its presence in the soul. Yet we doubt not but it is present in the minds of at least some few of us.

It is safe to say that no such question would enter our minds if at this time we were being persecuted because of the faith, as were the early Christians in the Roman Empire, or the Protestants in Reformation days. For them it was just natural to long for their redemption in the day of Christ. The world's offscouring, they looked ahead with fervent anticipation to the day of their perfect victory over the world. Victims of gross injustice, they prayed with strong crying and tears for their early justification in the sight of all. Innocently condemned by the world, oft-times to death, they liked to think of themselves as sitting in judgment upon the world.

Who would dare to find fault with them for this? Did not the Saviour express a like sentiment when he stood on trial before the Jewish Sanhedrin? Fully aware that he was about to be condemned, he was comforted by the thought that one day the tables would be turned: he would sentence the members of this council. Therefore he exclaimed exultingly, 'Hereafter shall ye see the Son of man sitting on the right hand of power, and coming in the clouds of heaven' (*Matt.* 26:64). Then why should not the sixteenth-century Christian have derived this comfort from Christ's return to judgment: 'That in all my sorrows and persecutions, with uplifted head, I look for him who shall cast all his and my enemies into everlasting condemnation, but shall translate me with all his chosen ones to himself, into heavenly joys and glory' (*Heidelberg Catechism*, Q. 52)?

Neither would we think it at all selfish to regard the Saviour's advent from the viewpoint of our own redemption if today we were subject to the bitter persecution of the faithful followers of the Christ which, according to the chapter from which our text is taken, will shortly precede the end. Heartily would we sympathize with the souls of the martyred saints under the altar, as they cry out with a loud voice, 'How long, O Lord, holy and true, dost thou not judge and avenge our blood on them that dwell on the earth?' (*Rev.* 6:10).

Even today we ought to look forward with feverish longing to the time of our redemption. To be sure, just now there seems to be a lull in the conflict between the woman's seed and the serpent's. We are enjoying a breathing-spell. But believe us, the fight is still on. 'In the world ye shall have tribulation', said the Master to the twelve (*John* 16:33). But that prediction was meant to be of very wide application. It holds for all of Jesus' disciples of every age. We hesitate not to affirm that tribulation at the hands of the world is a mark of Christianity. 'The servant is not greater than his lord. If they have persecuted me, they will also persecute you' (*John* 15:20). 'If *any* man will come after me, let him deny ·himself, and take up his cross, and follow me' (*Matt.* 16:24). These unequivocal statements of our Lord prove the point.

That the world today can put up with us so very well is in a measure at least, due to our unfaithfulness. If we were better Christians; if, as Christians, we boldly testified against the world, it would not be long before the world would lay violent hands on us. And then we too would watch, more eagerly than watchmen for the morning, for the bursting upon us of the day of our redemption. And oh! what unspeakable comfort the sure knowledge of the coming of that day would impart to our heaving souls!

Sometimes the redemption of man and the glory of God are spoken of in contrast with each other. It is not well to contrast the two. How greatly God will be glorified in the redemption of his people at the last day!

The opposing armies in the conflict of the ages have each its own commander. Satan is leader of the sons of men. The Son of God is the *Generalissimo* of the sons of God. The redemption of God's people will of course mean their victory. Now is it not true that the general of a victorious army usually receives the honour of the triumph gained? Of the final and complete triumph at the end of the ages, Christ will receive *all* the honour. Justly so! Not even with his army will he have to share it. For when his army seems crushed, the Son of God, appearing in the clouds, will turn defeat into victory. He will be crowned Lord of all.

And is not the church the body of Christ? Will not the redemption of the body necessarily enhance the glory of the Head?

'He that toucheth you toucheth the apple of [God's] eye' – thus an ancient prophet comforted the people of Jehovah (*Zech.* 2:8).

When God avenges his people, he will avenge the apple of his eye. When God redeems his people, he will redeem his own honour.

All that will come to pass. Of this the Christian is certain. His redemption, God's glorification, will be the end of history. The future is his. The end is God's. And that means that the child of God cannot be anything but an inveterate optimist.

b. There is a great deal of extremely superficial optimism in the world today. Half the world is telling the other half to keep smiling and not to worry. If you take a dark view of general conditions on earth, you are sure to have somebody repeat in your ears the words of Browning which have already been repeated so often that they have become nauseating, 'All's right with the world.' The trouble with the optimism of our day is that it deliberately shuts its eyes to dark realities, in happy-go-lucky fashion laughs unpleasant truths out of court, in cheerful lying calls black white. Surely, such optimism is sickening.

The beauty of Christian optimism is that it faces the truth, the whole truth, even the most unpleasant truth, without losing one bit of its brightness. That is optimism worth the while.

What does Jesus mean by 'these things'? He has been speaking of several signs of his coming, all of them belonging to the class usually designated *unfavourable.* False teachers; wars, earthquakes, famines and pestilences; persecution of the faithful; alarming signs in nature, are some of the things he mentioned. Now, by way of conclusion and practical application, he says: 'When these things begin to come to pass, then look up, and lift up your heads; for your redemption draweth nigh.' Are 'these things' the special signs in nature, the shaking of the powers of heaven, spoken of last; or is the reference to all the signs mentioned in the discourse? For our present purpose it does not make a great deal of difference how we answer this question. In either case our text speaks of a beautiful manifestation of Christian optimism. Yet it seems to us that the latter interpretation is the better of the two. It strikes us as being somewhat arbitrary to limit the reference of 'these things' to the last of the signs named. We take it that the Master is thinking of all.

Darkness may reign; the smoke of battle may hang over the face of the earth in formation so dense as to hide the sun; earthquakes may transform in a moment's time brilliant cities into tumbling ruins; famine may render the best kept bodies of men black with leanness; the Black Death may run through the world like a madman; the fair face of the beautiful earth may be turned into one large burial place; – the Christian strolls through this cemetery, posture erect, head uplifted, face beaming.

The church of the living God may rock upon its foundations; false teachers may lead out untold professing Christians; the world may feed the flesh of the faithful few to the fiercely flaming fire; the body of Christ on earth may face apparent annihilation; the Christian sings:

> A river flows whose streams make glad
> The city of our God,
> The holy place wherein the Lord
> Most high has his abode;
> Since God is in the midst of her,
> Unmoved her walls shall stand,
> For God will be her early help,
> When trouble is at hand.
>
> PSALM 46.

The Christian himself may be assailed: men may laugh him to scorn, even crowd him out of the world; his own brother may deliver him unto death; he may be burned up, cast to the wild animals, sawn asunder – his song of victory will be heard above the grating of the saw, the roaring of the lions, the crackling of the fire.

All nature may be turned topsy-turvy: the sun may be changed into sackcloth and the moon into blood; the stars may fall from their courses; the roaring waves of ocean may deluge whole lands; so that scientists are dumbfounded, and from fright fly into insanity – the Christian's serenity will be like that of a suckling at its mother's breast.

That is optimism for you.

The Christian retains his optimism *in spite of* unfavourable signs. Better than that, the Christian's optimism is manifested more and more as the unfavourable signs increase in number and in unfavourableness. The more reason he seems to have to hang his head in despondency, the higher does he lift his head in joyous hope. The deeper the darkness round about him, the brighter the light within the Christian's heart. For the clouds that lower on every side tell him of the early descent of the cloud on which his Redeemer will ride. And black darkness everywhere spells for him the present bursting of eternal day.

The Christian is optimistic *because of* the unfavourable signs of the times; surely not because of these signs as mere events of the day, but because of these signs *as signs*.

That is the very acme of optimism.

THAT IS CHRISTIAN OPTIMISM.

When Jesus tells his followers to look up and to lift up their heads, does he mean to imply that they should no longer concern themselves in any way with things earthly, that they should desist from all activity in the various spheres of mundane life, cease even from their daily occupations, as did the Christians at Thessalonica in apostolic days; in a word, let the world perish?

That cannot be his meaning. Since Christians will never know the exact day of the Saviour's return, they will have to continue their vocations to the end. As long as Christians have a natural body, they will have to concern themselves with things natural.

And as long as they are in the world, they will have a duty toward society.

But as the end draws nigh, the followers of the Christ will practically be forced out of the world. Their foes will crowd them to the wall. It will be next to impossible for them to make as much as a living. Further attempts to save the world from utter ruin will appear wholly futile.

Yet even then – and now again observe the Christian's indomitable optimism! – when he can no longer do anything for society, he will not yet despair of its salvation. From earth he will look up to heaven, from himself to the Son of God. What the Christian cannot do, the Christ can do. The Christian knows that the Christ *will* do it. Presently he will snatch God's creation as a firebrand out of the fire. A new earth will he establish, in which righteousness dwells.

c. That the Christian's optimism will be justified in the end is a foregone conclusion. God himself guarantees it. So we need not dwell on that particular point. But we do wish to dwell on the truth that we may expect this justification *at an early date.*

May we speak of the *early* justification of the Christian's optimism? After all, are we so certain that Jesus is coming *soon?* We reply that, though, for all we know, he may tarry another thousand years or even more, yet it is our *duty* to look for him at an early date.

Evidently Jesus desired his followers in every age to look for his speedy return. It was his wish that not a single generation of Christians should ever fall asleep or even slumber, thinking that the great day was still distant. Jesus wanted all his followers ever to be on the alert. For that reason the signs which he mentioned of his coming; though they are sufficiently definite; though, when the end has come, all will agree that they were exceedingly definite; yet are not so definite as to forbid the Christians of every age, from the apostolic down to our own, to conclude that the Saviour might very well come in the near future. Though Jesus did not actually come in their days, still past generations of Christians were right in supposing that he might come speedily. Jesus himself wanted that thought to control them. It controlled his apostles already. Divinely inspired, they wrote as if the end were imminent. They thought it was. And Jesus wants the same thought to control us. Therefore, when he bade the twelve watch for his return, he added, 'What I say unto you, I say unto *all*, WATCH' (*Mark* 13:37). And does not God's special revelation end with the *standing* announcement, 'Surely I come QUICKLY' (*Rev.* 22:20).

Now if, in addition to this general truth, we consider the exceedingly rapid multiplication of wonderfully striking signs in our own day, which was at least suggested by this series of sermons, then we are confirmed in the conviction that we *may* not merely, but positively *must*, look for the Saviour's *early* appearance.

Is it not possible that God will give an unexpected turn to the course of events, and then allow the history of our race to continue for a long period to come? No one can with certainty deny the possibility. For aught we know, the world may stand another nineteen hundred and nineteen years or more. But that should not be our first concern. It is not our affair. The secret things belong to the Lord, our God. We have to do with what has been revealed in his Word. We must study the signs of the Saviour's advent as stated in the Word. And when we plainly see these signs in our own day, we *must* conclude that God's day is hasting.

Our chapter makes mention of two signs of which we see but little, if anything, in our day. But, as will presently be pointed out, we may expect them to come to pass at almost any time. And from the context it is perfectly plain that, when they actually do appear, the Son of God will appear almost simultaneously. We have reference to the final persecution of the saints and the shaking of the powers of heaven.

Do you see no signs of the coming persecution? But the consolidation of humanity under Antichrist, now well under way, is sure to issue in the bitterest kind of persecution of God's elect. Who has not read of the brutalities to which the church is being subjected in the lands in which Bolshevism has gained the upper hand? We are aware, are we not, of a movement on foot in the State of Michigan to crush our free Christian schools? It now seems certain that in November 1920 the people of this state will decide at the polls whether or not all children to the age of sixteen will be compelled to attend the public schools. In some other states of the Union, hatred of Christian schools seems at least as rife. Masonry, we fear, stands behind it all. There are cities in free America where a man can hardly make a living unless he join a labour union. If a Christian for conscience' sake refuses to join a certain union and yet persists at his occupation, he is in grave peril of being clubbed, perhaps to death. Does it not sometimes look as if our Christian women may soon be compelled to exercise the right of suffrage, which is everywhere being extended to them,. and be forced into various kinds of public service? The sovereignty of the church in its own spiritual sphere is being menaced seriously.

There is a strong tendency, even in our own sweet land of liberty, to give the government some say about matters in which only Jesus Christ, the King of the church, has authority. In the course of the war this tendency has grown very strong. The abrupt closing of many churches during the influenza epidemic at least suggests the trend affairs are taking. It has become a common thing for ministers of the gospel to have sermon topics, even texts, suggested to them by the government. Some of these suggestions are actually accompanied by sermon outlines. The day of tribulation is coming. Do we go too far when we assert that it is *hasting?*

The powers of heaven are not yet being shaken. Some very nervous and imaginative people sometimes think they are. Several were on edge when, a few years ago, Halley's Comet could be seen. Of course they were mistaken. Yet who can say how soon the powers of heaven may actually be shaken? This sign of all signs will come unheralded.

Finally, be it known that the persecution of the saints and the disturbance of nature will, in part at least, be simultaneous. The former will not be over when the latter commences. And the latter will not be over, when Christ appears.

Now do you still ask whether it is permissible to speak of the *early* justification of the Christian's optimism?

Is the return of the Son of God going to mean *your* redemption? That question you must answer. If you cannot answer it affirmatively, you cannot be an optimist. You may tell yourself not to worry, but you have reason to worry. You may try to keep smiling, but you have cause for weeping. If you are not prepared to meet the Christ, tremble! When he makes his appearance, you too will look up and lift up your head; however not because you wish to, but because you cannot help it. Not wishing to see him, not able to bear the sight of him, you will beg the mountains and the hills to cover you. Do kiss the Son then, while it is called today, lest you perish on the morrow! Seek redemption from your sins in his blood now! Then he will redeem you from the world at his coming presently.

Our text is a command. We are *commanded* to look upward for the coming Redeemer. The command is not superfluous. Christians there be who stare and stare and stare, until they are almost blind, at the unfavourable signs of the times. If at moments they do look up, it is with blurred vision. They sigh and weep about the dark times in which they live; they fail to sing of the coming redemption of the children of God. These Christians are not sufficiently Christian. If they were better Christians, they would obey the Master's command to look up and lift up their heads. *If they were better Christians, they would be greater optimists.*

Do you think yourself a Christian, and yet do you dread the great day? Very likely you are not treading the pathway of sanctification as faithfully as you ought. 'Beloved, seeing that ye look for such things, be diligent that ye may be found of him in peace, without spot, and blameless' (*2 Pet.* 3:14). 'And now, little children, abide in him; that, when he shall appear, we may have confidence, and not be ashamed before him at his coming' (*1 John* 2:28).

If you diligently heed these exhortations, then, in answer to your Saviour's voice coming to you with clarion clearness in the signs of the times, 'SURELY I COME QUICKLY', you may exclaim with heart aflutter and lips trembling with ardently joyous anticipation, 'EVEN SO, COME, LORD JESUS' (*Rev.* 22:20).

AMEN.